O9-BTL-791

A CHRISTIAN'S GUIDE TO ISLAM

Smyth & Helwys Publishing, Inc.
6316 Peake Road
Macon, Georgia 31210-3960
1-800-747-3016
©2008 by Smyth & Helwys Publishing
All rights reserved.
Printed in the United States of America.

The paper used in this publication meets the minimum requirements of
American National Standard for Information Sciences—
Permanence of Paper for Printed Library Materials.
ANSI Z39.48–1984. (alk. paper)

Library of Congress Cataloging-in-Publication Data

McCullar, Michael, 1954–
A Christian's guide to Islam / Michael McCullar.
p. cm.
ISBN 978-1-57312-512-3 (alk. paper)
1. Islam. 2. Islam—Doctrines. I. Title.
BP161.3.M4 2008
297.02'427—dc22
2008001208

A CHRISTIAN'S GUIDE TO

GUIDE TO

Islam

MICHAEL McCULLAR

TABLE OF CONTENTS

PROLOGUE

With more than one billion adherents, Islam is the second largest religion in the world. To place this into perspective, Christianity has two billion followers and is seven hundred years older than Islam. One in every five people on Earth is a Muslim, and the majority of those live in places other than the Middle East. Succinctly stated, Islam is pervasive and reaches into every corner of the world. Islam is also difficult to characterize, especially when contrasted with Christianity, as it is more than a religion in the conventional sense. Noted Middle East scholar Bernard Lewis sums up the uniqueness of Islam: "In one sense Islam denotes a religion, a system of belief and worship; in the other, the civilization that grew up and flourished under the aegis of that religion. The word Islam thus denotes more than fourteen centuries of history, a billion and a third people, and a religious and cultural tradition of enormous diversity" (3).

Islam's initial impact within Arabia focused on a quest for monotheism and social and economic equity. Mired for centuries in a divisive tribal mentality, Arabia was violently fragmented and highly polytheistic. It was into this culture that Muhammad brought his initial message of peace, equality, and the worship of the one High God. Universally rejected in Mecca, he took a small band of followers to Medina and altered his teaching to include sanctioned fighting for Allah's will to be accomplished. This shift in theology and practice propelled Muhammad and Islam into power in Arabia and created a mindset of holy conquest. Soon after subduing Arabia, Islam came to see the world in two spheres—the House of Islam (the part of the world adhering to Islam) and the House of War (the part of the world not yet under Muslim control and influence). The overriding purpose of Islam would become bringing the world under the dominion of Islam. To this end, jihad or holy war became a companion of the

Muslim and remains at the crux of Islam. To how high a degree has each of these tenets been misinterpreted, corrupted, or abused over the centuries? Is jihad the single most alienating component of Islam in the eyes of the West? Is today's violent minority representative of Islam as a whole? What is the future for the world's fastest growing religion in the East?

This book has been created to deal with each of these questions in ways both frank and fair. While I wrote this book from a distinctly Western view, I have genuinely attempted to be nonpartisan and open. To this end, I spent time with Muslim scholars in Europe and the United States, as well as with Western Muslims who are living assimilated lives while continuing to practice their faith. I also invested time among former Muslims who now embrace Christianity as their faith expression. The result of this "balanced" endeavor to understand Islam and to relate to Muslims and former Muslims is an honest look at the state of Islam in the twenty-first century. My primary goal has always been to be both nonpartisan and "middle-of-the-road."

The world seems to be nearing a tipping point in relation to Islam. There is much fault to be shared, and truth be told, the majority of the fault seems to be genuine to Islam. Radical Muslims have captured the world's attention, and their acts virtually define modern Islam for much of the West. This is an incorrect definition of Islam as a whole, but often perception defines reality. As long as those in the West *perceive* that Islam is a religion of radicalism, dialogue and relational progress will be impossible. This book is an attempt to provide a brief but accurate guide to Muslim formation, history, structure, beliefs, practices, and goals. My hope is that knowledge will lead to relationships and dialogue between Christians and Muslims.

It is painfully obvious that portions of Islam are at war with both the West and with other Muslims. Killing is a daily occurrence and the motive for each death, regardless of who pulls the trigger, seems to end up being related to God. Is this proper theology for any religion? This has been and will continue to be a divisive question. Dialogue, however, will open doors and make it possible to find common ground. Is it possible to dialogue with a radical Islamist, especially over the character of God? Likely not, but six million Muslims live in the United

States and most are *not* radical in any sense of the word. The first step is to understand Islam; the second step is to build relationships with Muslims; and the third step is to stand together for a world where peace triumphs over war carried out in the name of God. This book is dedicated to the purposes of knowledge, dialogue, and the pursuit of peace in God's name.

CHAPTER ONE

Muhammad

Muhammad, the founder of Islam, was born in Mecca, the center of polytheistic worship in Arabia. The exact date of his birth is unknown as ancient Arabs did not seem to value such information, but he was probably born no later than 570 CE. Muhammad's father was named Abdullah, which means "servant of Allah." This name suggests that Muhammad's ancestral tribe worshiped Allah, the god above all gods in the pantheon of Arabic deities. This is an important point as it counters the arguments that Muhammad created a new religion: "Muhammad's father's name is important, showing that Allah, the Islamic name for God, was not coined by Muhammad, but was already in use for the Creator God" (Cotterell, 13). Muhammad's mother was named Aminah, a word meaning "peaceful" in Arabic. Muhammad was born into the Hashim clan, which was a part of the largest and most powerful tribe in Arabia, the Quaraysh. Muhammad's people were formerly Bedouins who had settled in Mecca where they became successful running caravan and livestock businesses. It is interesting to note that the Hashemite clan traced their ancestry back to Abraham and Ishmael.

Muhammad had an unsettled childhood that began with the death of both parents, his father shortly before his birth and his mother when he was six years old. These events left him an orphan and caused him to forfeit his father's estate. Shortly after his mother's death, he went to the desert to live with a Bedouin foster family. For a short time after that, he lived with his grandfather, the custodian of the *Kaa'bah*. Upon the death of his grandfather, he was sent to live with Abu Talib, an uncle who ran an extensive caravan business. The young Muhammad often traveled with these caravans to places outside of Arabia. It is almost certain that he visited Palestine, Syria, and Yemen, all places that held large Jewish and Christian populations. It is taught that on one of these trading trips Muhammad was stopped by a Syrian Christian monk who recognized him as Shiloh, the non-Jewish prophet mentioned in Genesis 19:1-10. Many believe that this event was the beginning of Muhammad's religious bent and that he was greatly influenced by the many Jews and Christians he met on these journeys. It is also possible that this odd encounter led Muhammad to become a religious mystic in his twenties and thirties (when he spent weeks in the mountains in meditation and isolation). There is little doubt that Muhammad was influenced by Syria's unity centered on the worship of one God. This was in stark contrast to Arabia's multiplicity of deities.

By the age of twenty-five, Muhammad had become both skilled and experienced in the caravan business. A wealthy Meccan widow named Khadijah hired him to lead one of her trading caravans into Syria. Muhammad's experience with the route and his knowledge of the Syrians led to many successful trips. As Sardar and Malik write, "Muhammad's courtesy, honesty and devotion to his work, earned the admiration of the widowed Khadijah. So impressed was she with the young Muhammad that she proposed marriage. Muhammad accepted. At age 40, she was 15 years older than him" (10). Khadijah's wealth and status allowed for Muhammad to pursue a more leisurely life and a higher rank in the Meccan society. Together they had four daughters, and by all accounts they enjoyed a close relationship marked by fidelity and adoration. After twenty-five years of marriage, Khadijah, the first convert to Islam, died at age sixty-five.

THE PROPHET

Muhammad's marriage to Khadijah and new status provided opportunity for many hours of isolated contemplation in the caves of Mount Hira. The exact nature and focus of Muhammad's spiritual retreats are not known, but theories abound. Muslim scholars believe these early retreats were preparation for the future revelations from Allah that would mark Muhammad as the final prophet. Peter Riddell and Peter Cotterell of the London School of Theology believe Muhammad's contemplation focused on all he had seen in Syria and what that might mean to his Arab people (21). In this vein it is possible that Muhammad was intrigued by the differences of the ordered and unified monotheism of the Syrian Christians and Jews and the divisive and fragmented polytheism of the tribal Arabs of his country. Karen Armstrong, author of many works on Islam, sees Muhammad simply following his spiritual duty during the Arab holy month of Ramadan, and indicates that he would not have been alone in following such a spiritual practice.

> Each year Muhammad retired with his wife and family to a cave on Mount Hira in the Meccan valley to make a spiritual retreat. This was quite a common practice in the Arabian peninsula at that time: Muhammad would have spent the month in prayer and would have distributed alms and food to the poor who came to visit him during this sacred period. (45)

Islamic writer Caesar Farah believes Muhammad was already a worshiper of *al-Llah* (later changed to Allah, Arabic for God), the highest deity in the Arabic pantheon and also the God of the "People of the Book," the Jews and Christians. According to Farah, the sequestered Muhammad would contemplate both the nature of Allah and the plight of his own people.

> The injustices permeating all levels of Meccan society in his days undoubtedly weighed heavily on his mind and caused him much anguish. The wealthy lorded over the poor; the helpless were at the mercy of the strong; greed and selfishness ruled the day; infanticide was widely practiced by Bedouins who lacked adequate means of sustenance, and there were numerous other practices prevailing on all levels of Arabian society that had the effect of widening the gulf between the privileged aristocracy and the deprived multitudes of Mecca. With such considerations preying on his mind, Muhammad found himself confronted by a twofold crisis: spiritual and social. (38)

Muhammad's annual Ramadan retreat radically changed in the year 610 CE. The then forty-year-old Muhammad was in a cave on Mount Hira when he received what he later understood to be a prophetic call. The angel Gabriel spoke to Muhammad with the words that form Sura 96:1-5 of the Qur'an. Muslims believe that during the experience, Muhammad "surrendered" control of himself and began to speak the actual words of Allah. Understandably, this encounter with Gabriel left Muhammad shaken to the point of becoming physically ill. Upon relating his experiences to his wife, he wondered if he had become possessed by the Arabic evil spirits known as *jinn*. The belief of a dark element filled with marauding and malevolent spirits was rich in Arabic religious lore. Khadijah assisted Muhammad in understanding the reality of his calling, even bringing in her Christian cousin, Waraqa ibn Nawfal, for counsel. Waraqa was familiar with Jewish and Christian Scripture, and it is taught that he declared Muhammad to be a truly called prophet along the lines of Moses.

Over time Muhammad made peace with his newfound calling as Allah's prophet and preached a message of monotheism and unity. The name of this new movement became Islam, the practice of "submission to the will of Allah." Those who "submitted" were called Muslims. Craig Chapman, author of *Cross and Crescent*, defines Islam as

> surrender to the will of Allah and obedience to his commands. It is a complete way of life. It tells a man about the purpose of his creation and existence, his ultimate destiny, his place among other creatures and, most importantly, it provides him with guidance to lead a balanced and purposeful life which will enable him to avoid the Hell-fire and be rewarded with a place in Paradise in the life after death. (69)

REVELATIONS

Muhammad's first revelation through the angel Gabriel came in 610 CE, and throughout the remaining 23 years of Muhammad's life he

received 114 additional revelations. These revelations were later collected and combined to form the *Qur'an*, Arabic for "recitation." It is
taught that Muhammad was illiterate and that few of the revelations
were formally recorded. Most were memorized and passed along
orally. It was not until after the death of Muhammad that the official
process of compiling the Qur'an began.

Muhammad's message was based on the revelations and formed a
simple but greatly unpopular message: "At the heart of the Qur'an is
the simple, repetitive warning that mankind must renounce paganism,
accept Allah as the One God of all mankind and live according to His
laws" (Horrie and Chippendale, 18). For three years he shared his new
message primarily with members of his clan and tribe, garnering many
more enemies than converts. The notion of moving away from paganism and seeking unity among all peoples would have had chilling
economic effects on most of Arabic society, especially among the elite
Quarysh tribe. Muhammad's own people controlled the annual pil-
grimages to the *Kaa'bah* and had become wealthy due to tribal
affiliations to the many gods of Arabia. Needless to say, Muhammad
was declared mad and dismissed as a fool. However, as his converts
grew in number, the persecution became material as a boycott of all
Muslim businesses was instituted, leading most Muslims to go into
temporary exile.

CELESTIAL JOURNEY

The year 619 CE was a pivotal one for both Muhammad and Islam. It
was during that year that Muhammad's wife, Khadijah, died, as well as
his uncle and tribal supporter, Abu Talib. Despite the fact that Abu
Talib never converted to Islam, he did protect Muhammad from the
full wrath of the powerful Quarysh tribe. This was also the year of the
infamous Night Journey. Islam teaches that while Muhammad was
sleeping near the *Kaa'bah*, he was transported by Gabriel on a celestial
journey. He was first taken to the temple site in Jerusalem, then
through the Seven Heavens where he visited with all the former
prophets, including Abraham, Moses, and Jesus. Some Muslims
believe that Gabriel also took Muhammad to the gates of Hell where

he witnessed the plight of the damned. Geisler and Saleeb, authors of *Answering Islam*, write that "Finally he was taken into the presence of God where he received the specific procedures for the Islamic worship of daily prayers" (75).

Geisler and Saleeb also report that news of the celestial journey led many close to Muhammad to question his truthfulness: "The news of this fantastic mystical experience led to an increase in the hostility of the Meccan opposition, and even many of the faithful began to doubt their prophet's truthfulness" (75). With his support slipping among his followers and having lost his uncle as tribal protector, Muhammad had to leave the holy city. That opportunity came in 621 CE when a delegation of men from the city of Yathrib (later renamed Medina, "the City of the Prophet") asked Muhammad to move to their city and assist in arbitrating tribal disputes. The following year the Muslims left Mecca for Medina, an event memorialized as the *Hijra*, or the Emigration; the year of the *Hijra* became Year One of the Muslim calendar (with dates marked as A.H., "after the *Hijra*").

The Medinan years saw Muhammad's stature grow as both a spiritual leader and civic organizer. He was successful in settling disputes among the various tribes and over time led many of them to convert from paganism to Islam. The revelations he received while in Medina also took on a different tone as the more functional aspects of the religion took precedence. John Renard, author of *Responses to 101 Questions on Islam*, writes,

> Muhammad's years in Medina, reflected in the text of the Qur'an as well as in later historical writing, witnessed major changes in his style of leadership and in the shape of the community of believers. Muhammad's prominence in the new setting gave prestige to the community. As the group increased, so did the demands on Muhammad's administrative time and skill, so that what began as spiritual leadership gradually grew into a more comprehensive oversight. (7)

The Medinan years also saw the shift from peace and unity to an atmosphere of conflict and war. Bolstered by almost total support in

Medina, Muhammad set out to align the Bedouin tribes who migrated in and around the city. This tactic followed the classic practice of Arabic warfare strategy—short-term confederations focused on a specific conquest with a promise of shared booty. Over the next six years Muhammad converted and aligned a massive army of followers and warriors; he set his sights on conquering his former tribe and, more importantly, the holy city of Mecca. The need for funds led the Muslims to begin to raid caravans, even during the heretofore sacred and holy weeks to which all Arabic religions adhered. This breech with Arabic spiritual practice led to another setback among many of Muhammad's backers but paved the way for the practice of jihad. The unique Islamic concept of jihad focused on the individual's struggle to align holistically with Allah's will. In essence it is the practice of "remembering" Allah. Rudolph Peters defines jihad as "To strive, to exert, or to struggle. The word has a basic connotation of an endeavor towards a praiseworthy aim, or to struggle against one's evil inclinations or to convert unbelievers for the sake of Islam" (1).

The Medinan battles led Muhammad to new revelations that expanded jihad to fighting for Islam, defending and progressing the faith through war. The Qur'an began to allow for warfare to protect and defend Islam from those who would threaten the *umma* (brotherhood of all Muslims) or restrict Islamic progress. To some, the "lesser" jihad is war and the "greater" is inner purity. To others, these are reversed.

> They will question thee concerning the holy month, and fighting in it. Say: "Fighting in it is a heinous thing, but to bar people from God's way, Disbelief in him and the Holy Mosque, and to expel its people from it—that is more heinous in God's sight; and persecution is more heinous than slaying." (Sura 2:217)

Fighting in the name of Allah was initially restricted to defense of the *umma* and to righting previous wrongs done against the people of Allah. For both of these reasons Muhammad led his followers against his former tribe and the various Meccan armies. There were both great successes and grand failures, and the Battle of Badr was Muhammad's first great military victory. Outnumbered and outflanked, the Muslims had laid siege on a Meccan caravan filled with items they themselves had left behind during the *Hijra*. In what is commonly taught as a set of miracles, the small Muslim army defeated the greater Quraysh warriors at Badr near the Red Sea. Muhammad saw his stature grow through humbling his former tribe, and the result was that even more Bedouin former tribes converted to Islam. The following year the same armies fought again; this time, however, the outcome was entirely different in the second battle. At the Battle of Uhud the Quraysh defeated the Muslims when Muhammad's archers abandoned their positions. It was at this point that the Jews in Medina broke pacts of cooperation with Muhammad.

The large Jewish contingent in Medina was initially impressed with the message of monotheism and unity. Being strong monotheists living in a polytheistic and pagan society, the Jews bonded with Muhammad and aligned with him on many fronts. Peter Cotterell sees Muhammad as believing that he was proclaiming a restored Judaism and a reformed Christianity (17). Neither group yielded many Muslim converts; nevertheless, the majority of Jews supported Muhammad during the early period in Medina. The complete break came in 626 CE when Muhammad charged the Jews with siding with the enemies of Islam and with ridiculing him as being God's final prophet. His shifting stance on the Jews led him to change the prayer direction from Jerusalem to the shrine in Mecca, and to substitute Ramadan for Ashura (Hebrew atonement festival) as a holy time. In addition, Muhammad banished two Jewish tribes, and a third tribe was charged with conspiring with Muhammad's enemies. The penalty assessed against this tribe was historic for Islam, as the Hebrew men were executed and the women and children sold as slaves. This one dark event has been hard to defend by Muslims, especially in consideration of the Qur'anic stipulation of "no compulsion for religion" and "living at peace with the People of the Book." Tor Andre explains the rationale by citing the Jews as enemies of Allah and Islam:

> One must see Muhammad's cruelty toward the Jews against the background of the fact that their scorn and rejection was the great-

est disappointment of his life, and for a time they threatened com-
pletely to destroy his prophetic authority. For him, therefore, it was
a fixed axiom that the Jews were the sworn enemies of Allah and His
revelation. Any mercy toward them was out of the question.
(155–56)

In 630 CE Muhammad led a reported ten thousand warriors to the
gates of Mecca, presenting such overwhelming strength that the city
was taken without force. Muhammad went to the *Kaa'bah* on camel-
back and destroyed its many idols, rededicating it to the worship of
Allah. In the process he also provided for the shrine to continue to
receive the age-old *hajj*, but the annual pagan pilgrimage would now
be to worship only Allah during Ramadan. Additionally, Muhammad
solidified the *Kaa'bah*'s significance by linking it to the story of
Abraham, Hagar, and Ishmail. According to Muhammad, Allah's will
has always been for the Meccan shrine to be the holy ground of Islam.

In Arabic, Mecca means "the place of the drinking cup." Muslims
believe Hagar and Ishmail were driven away by Sarah and took
refuge in the desert. Struggling with thirst and hunger, Hagar called
upon God for help and a spring of water miraculously sprang from
the ground. Later Abraham and Ishmail met at that site and
together built a stone building to worship the One True God. This
is believed to be the origin of the Kaa'ba. (Dodge, 32)

EXPANSION

With all of Arabia under his control, Muhammad looked to neighboring countries for the expansion of Islam. Muslims considered this
expansion to be the expressed will of Allah. Muhammad viewed the
result of his prophethood as leading all of the non-Islamic world
(known as the House of War) to a submission to Allah, resulting in a
worldwide House of Islam. He sent correspondence to the leaders of
the Persian and Byzantine empires calling them to his new faith. To
Heraclius of Constantinople he wrote, "Now then I invite you to
Islam, embrace Islam and you will be safe; embrace Islam and Allah

will bestow on you a double reward. But if you reject this invitation of Islam, you shall be responsible for misguiding the peasants" (Bukhari).

Neither the Byzantines nor the Persians took Muhammad up on his offer for conversion, and in time Muslims conquered both groups. Islam used a simple strategy for dealing with other lands. Muhammad received a revelation (Sura 9:29) that Muslims should fight non-Muslims until they either accepted Islam or subjugation as second-class citizens who paid a tribute tax (*jizya*). Jews and Christians who accepted this second-class status were called *dhimmis*. This status of being both protected and "guilty" became the norm for several hundreds of years of imperial Islamic rule. Muhammad cited *dhimmis* as being guilty of receiving genuine revelations from Allah but over time perverting or forgetting them, as well as rejecting him as the final prophet.

Muhammad died in Medina as his forces were taking over Syria and Palestine. He had returned from a pilgrimage to Mecca when he fell ill, dying days later in June 632 CE at the age of sixty-three. Muhammad left neither successor nor plan for the future of Islam.

CHAPTER TWO

Rightly Guided Caliphs

SUCCESSORS

Muhammad died with no male children and left no plans for succession as leader of Islam. Many traditions of Islam state that Muhammad made a tacit choice for succession by privately telling Abu Bakr that he was to succeed him. Aisha (Muhammad's youngest and favorite wife of those he married after the death of his first wife, Khadijah) named him as the choice of Muhammad, and it is true that Muhammad selected him to lead prayers during his illness. Islam, however, had grown to include all of Arabia and was then made up of the early Meccan converts and those who became Muslim in Medina. It is possible that Islam's rapid expansion had become a looming problem that would, in time, do damage to the movement. That damage would become both real and clear as the choice was made as to who would succeed Muhammad as leader of all Islam.

FIRST SUCCESSOR

Abu Bakr was named to follow Muhammad as the second leader or first Rightly Guided Caliph of Islam. This choice was not without controversy as many within the community insisted that a blood relative should be the first successor. Ali ibn Abi Talib was the cousin and son-in-law of Muhammad and was one of the first converts to Islam. It was felt by many in the *umma* that as "family" of Muhammad he was the logical choice to succeed him. This would have been a very "Arabic" choice as it was felt that the blood tie between relatives was sacred. Plus, Ali was known for his charisma, piety, and writing skills. It was decided, however, that Ali was too young and inexperienced (Armstrong, 25), so the role of first successor went to Muhammad's assistant, Abu Bakr.

Abu Bakr presided over the continued expansion of Islam and the true coming together of *umma*. One early issue facing the movement was the idea that each area should have its own leader or guide (imam), but Bakr and Umar ibn al-Khattab (also a close companion of Muhammad) decided that no regressive move toward the ancient tribal system would occur. This choice led to the formation of a worldwide mindset for Islam. No longer fragmented by tribal allegiances, the Arabs were to exist under the umbrella of the *umma*. To this end, Bakr focused on the apostasy battles against renegade tribes who accepted Islam under Muhammad but were threatening to break away to return to their former structures. While most of these tribal defections were based on economics rather than theology, it was important for the totality of Islam to remain intact. Bakr was successful in holding the relatively new movement together. After two years of successful military conquests against the Persians and Byzantines, he fell ill and died.

SECOND SUCCESSOR

Umar ibn al-Khattab, close companion of both Muhammad and Bakr, and son-in-law of Muhammad, was selected as the next caliph. Once again there were Muslims who wanted Ali to succeed and bring the leadership back into the bloodline of Muhammad. Under Umar's leadership Islam conquered Iraq, Syria, and Egypt, and made progress in conquering the remainder of the Persian and Byzantine empires. Umar also created satellite garrison towns within the conquered lands so that rebellion and regressive change would be more difficult to achieve. Expansion came to be seen as a means of financial gain as all lands seized would also be plundered. At this point Islam was not yet focused on making converts outside of the Arabian Peninsula. The majority of non-Arabs encountered during Umar's time were Christians, who would have been resistant to actual conversion. Most Christians accepted *dhimmi* (second-class citizenship) status without great conflict, which allowed for Umar's reign to be of peaceful coexistence with the "People of the Book." Umar was assassinated in 644 CE by a Persian prisoner as he was praying in the mosque in Medina.

THIRD SUCCESSOR

The third caliph was Uthman ibn Affan. Under his leadership the expansion continued as Cyprus, portions of North Africa, Armenia, the Caucasus, Afghanistan, and portions of India all became Islamic land. By pure political standards, Uthman was a failure as he was prone to favor members of his own clan and those from Mecca over highly qualified candidates from Medina. This tendency toward nepotism, his unpopularity with his own military leaders, and his insistence that one standard version of the Qur'an be recited in faraway garrison towns led to a mutiny in 656 CE. There was also a consistent and growing call for Ali to lead the *umma*. It is taught that in the last days of Uthman's reign, Ali openly sided with those opposing the caliph. A group of soldiers returned to Medina to confront Uthman over their concerns and assassinated him in his home. After the death of Uthman, there was a widespread call for Ali to take the reins of leadership.

FOURTH SUCCESSOR

Ali's prominence, patience, and behind-the-scenes leadership had inspired a large following. Prominent members of Muhammad's clan, as well as the Companions (the early converts who migrated to Medina), called for Ali to become the fourth Rightly Guided Caliph. Their support was so pervasive that the group had become known as *Shi'atu Ali*, the Party of Ali. Soon this designation would shorten to the Shi'a party. After meeting with all operating factions within Arabic

Islam, Ali agreed to succeed Uthman and restore order to the maturing movement.

Ali's first and, in hindsight, worst move was to grant clemency to all those involved in Uthman's death. According to Reza Aslan, author of *No god but God*, Ali's time was to be one of forgiveness and reconciliation, not of retribution or reverting to old-style justice where "eye-for-an-eye" was mandatory (130). Ali also reversed Uthman's nepotistic appointments by removing all of Uthman's relatives from prominent positions. Ali's reign was destined to fail, however, as his clemency for those complicit in Uthman's assassination was too much to bear for many Muslims, particularly Muhammad's wife Aisha. While she hated Uthman and was reportedly involved in the deadly conspiracy to defeat him, she also did not support Ali as the ultimate Muslim leader. Along with two men she preferred as successors to her father Abu Bakr, Talha and Zubayr, she led an army of insurgents against Ali's forces in what has been termed the Battle of the Camel. This battle was Islam's first, but certainly not only, civil war, and marked the beginnings of a split that would define Islam for all of its history.

Initially the caliphate was seen as a secular position with a primary focus on keeping the *umma* together and overseeing the expansion of the movement. While the sitting leader would be following Muhammad in many ways, he would *neither be speaking for Allah nor acting as a prophet.* Up until the time of Ali's caliphate, this distinction was widely supported. However, as the factions grew within Islam, so did the expectations and duties of the caliph. This disagreement was fomented by the continuing expansion of Islam that had come to be seen by many as Allah's divine favor at work through the "correct" caliph. Again, this dichotomy between secular and religious leadership as an "either-or" proposition served only to advance the looming split between Muslims that would in time result in Shi'a and Sunni Islam.

Ali seemed determined to bring a truly pietistic model to the caliphate, even to the point of exerting full religious authority. This would have been an almost complete departure from the three earlier leaders, and was seen by many as an attempt to emulate Prophet Muhammad's unique role. Thus, the largest question facing Islam during the early tenure of Ali was which "type" caliph should lead the movement. Ironically, Islam never adequately dealt with this question, and the divide continued to widen as Ali's tenure progressed.

Ali's forces defeated Aisha's supporters at the Battle of the Camel, and Aisha was seriously wounded by an arrow. Rather than punishing her followers for insurrection, Ali "rebuked them and then pardoned Aisha and her entourage, allowing them to return to Mecca unmolested" (Aslan, 134). Ali's next battle was against the cousin of Uthman, Abu Sufyan, who held Ali responsible for the death of the third caliph. When close to a decisive defeat, Sufyan's army raised copies of the Qur'an on spears, which was a signal for surrender and arbitration. Ali's army had been loyal to their leader until this point, but a split emerged over his decision to allow for the rebels to be spared and given arbitration.

Many of Ali's supporters were from the Kharijite faction, an extreme group who saw the role of caliph primarily as Allah's spokesperson. The leader of the *umma* was to be the most spiritual and pious person in the full community regardless of ancestry or tribal affiliation. Rather than viewing a bloodline to Muhammad as prerequisite for being caliph, they focused on being "genuinely" Muslim. To this end the Kharijite's deemed the assassination of Uthman as being both necessary and a holy act on the grounds that he had broken the teachings of Allah. The Kharijite faction believed Uthman had forfeited his place as caliph and was no longer worthy of the position. Needless to say, the Kharijites are seen as the first "extreme" faction of Islam and as the first Muslim "theocrats."

The Kharijites were angry with Ali for sparing the army of Sufyan and allowing arbitration. Their most pointed criticism was focused on Ali's justifying his decision by citing the Qur'an (Sura 2:193). The arbitration rendered that the murder of Uthman was indeed foul and that retribution was allowed for. This decision seemed to quell Sufyan's rebellion, but it sealed Ali's fate with the conservative Kharijites, who now deemed Ali as unfit and unworthy under Muslim principles to lead Islam.

In short order Ali's remaining forces met the seceding Kharijites in battle. Ali's army won a decisive victory, but it would be his last as leader of Islam. While praying in the mosque, he was attacked by a Kharijite shouting, "Judgment belongs to God, Ali, not you." Ali suffered a head wound from a poisoned sword and died two days later. Ali's goal of bringing the caliphate back into the family line of Muhammad died along with him. However, to many Muslims of his time and to millions who would follow, Ali was more than the fourth caliph.

This heroic vision of Ali has been firmly planted in the hearts of those who refer to the person they believe to have been the sole successor to Muhammad not as the fourth caliph, but as something else, something more. Ali, the Shi'a claim, was the first imam: the Proof of God on Earth (Aslan, 136).

CHAPTER THREE

Sunni and Shi'a Islam

MUSLIMS DIVIDED

The schism that divided Islam has many points of origin, but the most prominent relates to the disagreements over Muhammad's direct successor. Muhammad left no official pronouncements or plans for Islam after his death. This fact alone led to great disagreement over who was the "right" person to become Muhammad's successor, the Rightly Guided Caliph. The group that came to be known as Shi'a believed that Muhammad had indeed assigned a successor, his cousin and son-in-law, Ali. They report that on his last pilgrimage to Mecca Muhammad stated, "For whoever I am leader, Ali is the leader." Muhammad died shortly thereafter, and the group who favored the Arabic practice of family succession felt that Ali was the only choice as successor to the Prophet.

The *umma*, or greater community of Islam, was quite large at this point, and leaders who had worked closely with Muhammad convened to select the next leader. This group chose Abu Bakr, one of Muhammad's closest companions and one of the true "elders" of the movement, as the first successor of the Prophet. Ali was thirty years of age and, consequently, was considered by many of the decision-makers to be too young and inexperienced for the role as leader of all Islam. The appointment of Abu Bakr as first Rightly Guided Caliph only

deepened the small but growing rift in Islam. The Shi'a faction, or
Shi'at Ali (Party of Ali), believed that Muhammad had definitely des-
ignated Ali as his successor and sought for all successors to be "People
of the House," or members of Muhammad's family. The Shi'a came to
view each of the first three successors as usurpers of Ali's rightful position as leader of the *umma*. This eventually led to the foundational
Shi'a belief that each of the first three successors were illegitimate and
that Ali was the first imam, or genuine successor of the Prophet.

The Shi'a imams are those who possess unique spiritual powers
and gifts. They are viewed as "infallible vessels of God's light" (passed
from the prophets to the imams), and are given the ability and responsibility to serve as intercessors between humankind and Allah. The
imam and later the position of ayatollah are seen by Shiite Muslims as
the ultimate "final say" for Islam and have both "God-derived and
God-related authority" (Bowker, 12). Imams and ayatollahs lead in
and through the mosque, and they exert almost supreme control of
Muslim states that have majority Shi'a populations.

The Shi'as and Sunnis disagree not only on who should have succeeded the Prophet, but also over the function his successor was to
play. Sunnis believe that the successor was succeeding *only* to the
Prophet's role as leader of the community. Shi'as believed that the true
successor was renewing and strengthening the bond between man and
God. The differences between Sunnis and Shi'as are thus not only
political but also theological and even anthropological (Nasr, 38–39).

The violent deaths of Ali and later his son, Husain, are corner-
stone events in Shi'a history that combine to create a mentality of
martyrdom and rebellion. The Umayyads took control of Islam after
Ali's assassination, and from that point forward the Shi'a have fought
an "intermittent 1,300-year war to overthrow the 'usurper' Umayyad
dynasty and the Sunni rulers who followed them and place Ali's
descendants back on the throne of a united Islamic empire" (Horrie
and Chippendale, 136). This mindset of defiance and of being historically wronged led to a perpetual civil war within Islam between the
minority Shi'as and the overwhelming Sunni majority. Since the seventh century, this has been a war without end that, in and of itself,
relinquishes the possibility of a "united Islamic empire."

SHI'A ISLAM

Unlike the Sunnis who were loyal to the duly empowered caliph, the Shi'as professed loyalty to an imam (leader or guide) who was a direct descendant of Ali through his son Husain, on the grounds that Ali allegedly had inherited from the Prophet both his spiritual and secular sovereignty, i.e., the power both to interpret and to enforce the canon law. This divine successorship comes first from Allah, then from his chosen mouthpiece Muhammad, then Ali, and finally his legitimate descendants (Farah, 178).

The largest subgroup within Shi'a Islam is called the Twelvers. Twelver Muslims believe that those in the line of Ali's offspring are divinely guided (even by the Prophet himself), are immune from sin and error, and hold the same authority as did Muhammad. The twelfth rightful successor of Ali was Muhammad ibn al-'Askari, who became imam at age four upon the death of his father.

The child imam mysteriously disappeared from his home in Iraq a few weeks later and was never located. As he had no brothers, the family line of succession from Ali ended. The majority of Shiites refused to believe al-'Askari died, preferring to believe that he supernaturally disappeared and is now at-large in the world in a concealed form. They believe that he will reemerge shortly before the end of the world as the *al-Mahdi*, or the "chosen one" referred to in the Qur'an. Twelver Muslims make up the majority of Iran and much of Iraq. The most fundamental Twelver Muslims believe that the return of the *Mahdi* can be sped up through a cataclysmic set of events that imperil the Islamic world.

Shiite Muslims teach that Muhammad thought the world would come to an end by 1100 CE at the latest. Since the world did not end, and the anticipated *Mahdi* did not appear, leadership of the Twelver sect passed to the *uluma*, a council of twelve elders selected on the basis of piety, scholarship, and leadership. Over the centuries the *uluma* has taken on more power and authority and has become synonymous with supreme leadership of both religion and state. The council also became judges and used *Shari'a* as the basis for all judgments. *Shari'a* is the all-encompassing Islamic law. As the power of these judges grew, the position of ayatollah was created. Today the ayatollah is seen as the divinely guided "imam-like" leader of Shi'a Islam.

In contrast to the Sunni Muslim majority, Shiite Muslims believe that Allah has complete foreknowledge of all human actions but does not predestine actions. The Shi'a follow the five pillars of Islam (described in chapter 5) as Sunni Muslims do, but have altered some of the prescribed practices. The call to prayer is different, as is the practice of three prayers each day rather than the Sunni practice of five daily prayers. Shiite Muslims allow for temporary marriages as was once allowed by Muhammad, even though he abrogated the practice before he died. They also venerate the tombs and shrines of imams, often to the point of superstitious worship, and are willing to conceal their beliefs to avoid persecution.

Shiite Muslims are the majority population and official religion of Iran (ancient Persia). Iraq's majority sect is also Shi'a, and it is home to two of the most important shrines of Shi'a Islam: the tombs of Husain in Karbala and Ali in Najaf. The differences between Shi'a and Sunni Muslims run so deeply that the two groups rarely worship in the same mosque.

SUNNI ISLAM

The term "Sunni" is derived from *sunna* and is an abbreviation of a longer term meaning "The People (*Sunna*) of Tradition and the Community." Sunni Islam values the concept of the *umma* and the overall cohesion of Islam. To this end, they represent the more inclusive of the branches of Islam and make up nearly 90 percent of the world's Muslims. Sunnis also view the Sunnah, a collection of six "authentic" books relating to the actions and sayings of Muhammad, as pivotal to their daily lives. The Sunnah instructs Muslims in much the same way that the Midrash assists the Jews.

Sunnis recognize four sources of spiritual authority:

The primary source is the Qur'an, considered as God's word given through Muhammad. Next to the Qur'an, the most important authority is the hadith. The word means the "news." The hadith are the traditions of what Muhammad did or said outside the Qur'an; they contain little direct information about the prophet's life and deeds. For situations not covered in the Qur'an and the hadith, there are two other sources. One is reasoning and the other is juristic opinion, which has in the course of time been replaced by consensus of jurists' opinions. (Ehlke, 41)

The four Sunni sources form the *Shari'a* and are considered the will of Allah for living as a Muslim. *Shari'a* is normally translated as "Islamic law." It is, however, not "law" but a set of regulations, principles, and values from which legislation and laws are drawn. While *Shari'a* is eternal, Islamic law—like all law—evolves and grows and continues to change as the Muslim situation changes (Sarder and Malik, 63). *Shari'a* is often simplified as "the Path" for Muslims to follow and is all-inclusive to daily living. Sunnis have advanced the position of legal scholars who interpret the four sources to determine application of shari'a. Sunni Islam acknowledges four orthodox schools of law. Each school is named for a particular jurist who was prominent during the formative years of growth and expansion. The four schools are the Maliki, Shafii, Hanafi, and Hanbali.

The Hanafi school is the largest and is considered the most liberal of all Sunni groups. The Hanbali school by contrast is widely seen as the most conservative (orthodox), as it stresses tradition and a literal reading of the Qur'an over reason. The Hanbali school is popular in Saudi Arabia and with the Baath party of Iraq, places that are seen as more regressive and restrictive. Shafii was the earliest jurist, and it was his groundbreaking study of the Hadith and his devotion to the life of Muhammad that laid the groundwork for the other schools. His work led to "the creation of a homogeneous religious life, based on the sacred law of the Shariah. The inspiration of the law was the person of the Prophet . . . by imitating the smallest detail of his external life and by reproducing the way he ate, washed, loved, spoke and prayed, Muslims hoped to be able to acquire his interior attitude of perfect surrender to God" (Armstrong, 60). Thus, Sunnis see themselves as being truly Muslim (surrendering to Allah) by practically prescribing to the life of Muhammad.

Sunnis also differ from Shi'a on religious hierarchy. In short, there is no formal clergy structure for Sunni Muslims. The consensus of the greater body (*umma*) is the prerequisite for decisions, and the function of imam is simply that of pious leader of prayer in the mosque. Where Shiite Muslims have a "home office" of sorts, the Sunnis do not. All Sunni Muslims are viewed as equals, and no intermediaries stand between the individual Muslim and Allah. The Sunni imam is not required to demonstrate a lineage from Muhammad; rather he must gain the support of the *umma*, the larger community of Sunni Muslims. Once the imam is elected, all Sunnis must follow the leader with unwavering support. Being a politically conservative sect and valuing the cohesion of the collective community, Sunnis are required to support the imam as long as he follows the *Shari'a* and is willing to wage jihad if Islam is attacked or threatened. Sunnis also believe in the return of the *Mahdi*, the mystical leader Allah will send to Earth to unite all Muslims into a single state/force as the end of the world nears. Sunnis also disagree with Shi'as over the unique identity of the *Mahdi*, and would therefore not recognize the "Twelfth" imam of Shi'a Islam.

CHAPTER FOUR

Qur'an

The Qur'an is the holy book of Islam. The term "Qur'an" literally means "recitation" or "readings." Muslims believe that Muhammad was given the content of the Qur'an in individual revelations over a period of twenty-three years: "It is We Who have sent down the Qur'an to you in stages" (Sura 76:23). Muslims do not believe, however, that Muhammad was the first person to receive God's revelations to humankind.

> The Islamic view of divine revelation is that in successive generations Allah revealed himself through prophets. The Muslim conviction is that each of these prophets (such as Moses or Jesus), although raised up in different eras, and in different communities, all had the same basic message: to call people to believe in the oneness of God, to submit to His law and do good works with the judgment of God in mind. (Orr-Ewing & Orr-Ewing, 8)

To this end, the Qur'an is believed to be the final revelation of Allah to humankind.

Over the final 23 years of his life, Muhammad received a total of 114 separate revelations. As Muhammad was reported to be illiterate, it is taught that he memorized each revelation. Over time assistants committed each revelation to memory and recorded them on whatever was at hand at the time. As described in the *Concise Encyclopedia of Islam*, "The Qur'an was collected from the chance surfaces on which it had been inscribed: from pieces of Papyrus, flat stones, palm leaves, shoulder blades and ribs of animals, pieces of leather, wooden boards, and the hearts of men."

With the death of Muhammad and many of those who had made it their role to memorize each revelation, it became important to compile a written and authoritative text. Over time questionable attributions to Muhammad surfaced, especially outside of Arabia, and many of the original Companions (the early converts who migrated to Medina) had died. The possibility of losing the very heart of the religion led Muhammad's first successor, Abu Bakr, to assign the standardizing of an authorized form of Allah's revelations. Bakr commissioned Zayd ibn Thabit to consult with other "memorizers," as well as compile all written fragments with the goal of producing a complete version of the Muslim holy text. This was a long process that culminated with Uthman, Muhammad's third successor, ordering Zayd to make copies of the authorized (canonized) Qur'an and distribute them to all places where Islam had spread.

It is easy to assume that the imprecise methods of recording the initial revelations, and the natural loss that occurs in oral traditions, might lessen the total authenticity of the text. Muslims believe quite the opposite, however, as the Qur'an is revered as being holy to the level of ink and stitching. Traditional Islam views the Qur'an as miracle and as manifestation of Allah. To defame the Qur'an is to defame Allah, both of which would be considered high heresy. Parshall writes, "Orthodox Islam generally affirms the uncreated Qur'an. Allah was and is preexistent to everything known and unknown. His word could no more be created than Allah himself could be created" (17). Muslims also believe that the Qur'an exists in Paradise as the "Mother" book, the Divine Reality. Whereas the Bible was an earlier revelation, it was corrupted by translations and is thus seen as inferior to the "Scripture whereof there is no doubt" (Sura 1:2).

As a book, the Qur'an itself is extremely difficult to read by Western standards. It is not arranged in chronological order, nor does it share the types of prose found in the Old or New Testaments. Those familiar with the Bible realize that it was written over a span of 1,500 years and is more of a library of books rather than a singular book. The Bible is arranged chronologically and by subject matter and was recorded in multiple languages. The Qur'an was revealed in Arabic to one person and was compiled over a relatively short period of time. So important was Arabic to the early Muslims that it was decreed that the only true Qur'anic rendering could be in the original language. To this day Muslim children worldwide are encouraged to read and memorize Qur'anic verses in Arabic. All other language versions are considered merely "interpretations."

Of the 114 suras (chapters) in the Qur'an, 86 are from Muhammad's time in Mecca. The other 28 were revealed during his time in Medina. Of course, an untrained non-Muslim reader would not readily understand the timeline of the Qur'an due to the unique arrangement of chapters. The text is not laid out in the chronological order in which Muhammad received them. If this had been the case, the first sura would be the first revelation received and the final sura would be the final revelation. In fact, the first revelation is in Sura 96 and the final revelation is in Sura 5. For the initiated Muslim reader, however, the 6,616 lines and 78,000 words of the Qur'an demonstrate Allah's monologue to humankind and hold the prescription for living in Allah's will. According to Ehlke, "Muslims look to the Qur'an almost as Christians look to Christ (John 1:1)—God's eternal Word that has come to earth" (58).

The early Meccan suras spring from the time of intense opposition from the large pagan tribes and thus focus on the oneness of Allah and the need to abolish idol worship. These suras also stress the need for personal piety and faith practice. The later Medinan suras came after Islam found traction in its new location and center on organizing the Muslims into an all-inclusive community of faith. These later suras detail moral and ethical codes, criminal law, economic and civic policies, and offer guides for relations with other communities. Again, it would seem that the earlier revelations were theological and the latter were lessons on social and civic matters. This would be a false assumption, however, as Islam is inclusive of all aspects of life. Christians and Jews view life through the lens of faith. Islam *is* life for the Muslim and cannot be separated from other areas of existence. Professor and writer Yusuf Ibish provides insight into the unique status of the Qur'an for Muslims:

I have not yet come across a western man who understands what the Qur'an is. It is not a book in the ordinary sense, nor is it comparable to the Bible, either the Old or New Testaments. It is an expression of the Divine Will. If you want to compare it with anything in Christianity, you must compare it with Christ Himself. Christ was the expression of the Divine Will. That is what the Qur'an is. If you want a comparison for the role of Muhammad, the better one in that particular respect would be Mary. Muhammad was the vehicle of the Divine, as she was the vehicle. The Qur'an was divinely inspired, then it was compiled, and what we have now is the expression of God's Will among men. (quoted in Waddy, 14)

There is an Islamic practice related to the Qur'an that is seen as questionable by non-Muslims. Qur'anic reading allows for abrogating or canceling verses that were revealed at an earlier time. For example, if Muhammad received a revelation while in Mecca, the content could be changed by a later revelation received in Medina. This obviously occurred several times as the Qur'an is filled with abrogated teachings. One of the most striking examples deals with relationships between Muslims and "The People of the Book," Christians and Jews. Sura 5 teaches Muslims to be both friends and enemies with Christians and Jews. Certain verses encourage peace and abstinence from violence unless provoked, while others strongly suggest the opposite: "But when the forbidden months are past, then fight and slay the pagans wherever you find them, and seize them, beleaguer them, and lie in wait for them in every stratagem of war" (Sura 9:5). This is known as the Sword Verse and is dated 731 CE. This would have been one of the final revelations received by Muhammad before his death in 732 CE and would have abrogated 124 previous verses teaching tolerance toward non-Muslims: "Let there be no compulsion in religion: truth stands out clear from error" (Sura 2:256).

THE OTHER HOLY BOOKS

The Hadith and Sunnah are instructional texts for Muslim living and serve as a guide or path to follow (*Sunnah* literally means "path"). The Sunnah is based on the conduct of Muhammad as both prophet and person, while the Hadith are the sayings and teachings attributed to Muhammad over his life as prophet. The Hadith and Sunnah are second only to the Qur'an as authoritative in Islam. It is important to note that Muhammad did not write the Qur'an, nor is it "his" teachings. Muhammad is seen as simply the conduit for Allah's final revelation to humankind. Both the Sunnah and Hadith, however, are strictly based on the examples and teachings of Muhammad.

The need for the aforementioned additional texts became clear after Islam had expanded to the point that the Qur'an alone could not answer its many issues. Reza Aslan writes, "As Muhammad's small community of Arab followers swelled into the largest empire in the world, it faced a growing number of legal and religious challenges that were not explicitly dealt with in the Qur'an" (67). Thus, an exhaustive search was undertaken to record and compile as many sayings and acts of Muhammad as possible, then seek to determine which were authentic. The leading Muslim scholar to undertake this task was Al-Bukhari, who spent sixteen years collecting more than 3,000 verified Hadith. Today the Sunnah and Hadith are often combined, and the titles are used interchangeably. Officially, however, the Sunnah refers to the acts of the Prophet and the Hadith is restricted to the sayings of Muhammad. There are presently 93 chapter topics within the authoritative combination of sayings and actions of Muhammad. A great portion of the *Shari'a* law has been compiled from these writings.

THE QUR'AN AND THE BIBLE

Islam regards the Hebrew and Christian scriptures as being "previously" authentic. Muslims teach that the Bible was God's earlier revelation through Abraham, Moses, and later Jesus, but as a whole it was either disregarded or corrupted. God's revelation through a later prophet, or in the view of Islam, a final prophet, is seen as humankind's final opportunity to return to God's original purpose. To this end, the Qur'an has many references to people, places, and events that are also found in the Bible, although the Qur'an treats most of these in ways dissimilar to the Bible. In the Qur'an, Abraham is seen as the father of Islam, just as Jews consider him the father of Judaism.

The differences between the Muslim and Hebrew accounts revolve around which son Abraham was willing to sacrifice in obedience to God. Isaac is the focal son in the Old Testament accounts. Muslims believe, however, that Ishmail was Abraham's primary son and that God used him to test Abraham's faith. Neither son is actually named in the Qur'anic account, but Muslims teach that for the first fourteen years of his life, Ishmail was Abraham's only son and is, thus, the "son" in question.

The Qur'an teaches that Ishmail and his mother, Hagar, were exiled into the desert by Abraham's jealous wife, Sarah. Facing death due to hunger and thirst, Hagar prayed that Allah would save them. As a part of her petition, Hagar ran back and forth between two hills. Muslims believe that Allah answered her prayer by sending forth a spring of water from the barren ground (Well of ZamZam). Hagar and Ishmail took this as a divine instruction to settle at that spot. This is reportedly how Ishmail became the father of the Northern Arabians and how Mecca became God's choice for a holy city. Muslims also believe that Abraham visited Ishmail there and together they rebuilt the ancient *Kaa'bah* (first built by Adam) as a place for ritual worship of Allah.

JESUS

The Qur'an and the Old Testament treat Moses in almost the exact manner. The same cannot be said for Jesus, however, as he remains the critical point of disagreement between Christianity and Islam. Coincidentally, Jesus is the crux of Christians' disagreement with Judaism as well. Ehlke sums it up this way:

> Christianity recognizes the Old Testament as inspired Scripture fore-telling the Messiah, the Christ, whose coming is reported in the New Testament. Judaism does not accept Jesus as the promised Savior and so rejects the New Testament. In theory, Islam accepts the Bible, but in practice it rejects the messianic nature of the Old Testament and its fulfillment in Jesus. (56)

The name *Isa* (Arabic for Jesus) occurs in 11 of the 114 suras, although many other indirect references exist in the Qur'an. Isa is bestowed with an amazing list of titles in the Qur'an, from Messiah to Word of God, with each reference denying that he was in any way divine. To the Muslim, Jesus is nothing more than one of the great prophets. Oddly, the virgin birth of Jesus is recorded in the Qur'an, but all divine aspects are rejected. Muslims do not consider Jesus to be sinless and view Adam as actually having the more miraculous birth. Sura 3:59 reads,

> Jesus, in God's sight,
> Is as Adam's likeness;
> He created Him of dust,
> Then said He unto him,
> "Be," and he was.

Muslims believe that the birth of Jesus was miraculous in that he had no earthly father. Adam, the first prophet, exceeds Jesus as he had neither human father nor mother.

Muslims also believe that Jesus declared his unique status as prophet in infancy. It is taught in Sura 19 that Mary went away to deliver the baby and did so under a palm tree. She became hungry and thirsty after delivery and was instructed by the infant to drink of a nearby stream and to shake a palm tree to enjoy fresh dates. Later in the same sura, Mary's family responds negatively to her unmarried pregnancy. She appeals to the infant child for wisdom.

> Mary pointed to the child then;
> But they said,
> "How shall we speak to one who is still in the cradle,
> A little child?"
> He said, "Lo I am God's servant;
> God has given me the Book,
> And made me a prophet . . . ." (vv. 29-30)

The Qur'an does not teach that Jesus was crucified. Muslims believe that he was simply "taken up to Paradise," and that he will figure prominently at the end of time. Muslim scholars do not agree upon his precise role at the end of time, but it is thought that he will signal the coming "Day of Judgment." Muslims agree that Jesus will return and afterward he will complete his human role and die. Muslims argue against the crucifixion of Jesus for two main reasons. First, to be hung on a cross is to die an accursed death, which would be impossible for a prophet. Second, Jesus prayed for deliverance, and the prayer of a prophet must be answered. All the discussions regarding the divinity-versus-mere-prophet status of Jesus delineate the point of separation between the two religions. Without the full divinity of Jesus, Christianity is hollow and void: "Once it is established that Jesus did not die on the cross, there was no accursed death, no bearing of the sins of mankind, no resurrection, no ascension and no atonement. The entire structure of church theology is thereby demolished" (Khan, 89).

The Qur'an also clashes with the New Testament in its treatment of the Trinity. At the heart of Islam is monotheism, the belief in one God. The history of pre-Islam Arabia is one of factionalized tribes worshiping a panoply of deities. Muhammad's core message was a return to the worship of the One true God, the God of Abraham and Jesus, and, subsequently, a rejection of all other gods and idols. Muslims thus wholly reject the uniquely Christian doctrine of the Trinity.

Islam deems the notion of Allah sharing stature or being separated into portions or persons as ultimate heresy. When combined with the belief that Jesus was a human prophet, and not in any form divine, it is easier to see the lines of core conflict. Those lines become murky, however, when the Muslim definition of the Trinity is explored. Rather than view the Christian Trinity as God the Father, God the Son, and God the Spirit, Muslims opt for God, Mary, and Jesus as the Trinity. Christians would concur that the inclusion of Mary yields an incorrect definition by standards of the New Testament. Muslims also believe that all Christians worship and deify Mary due to her unique state of "sinlessness" and the particulars of the Virgin Birth. Suras 4 and 5 demonstrate the theological divide between Christians and Muslims related to Jesus, Mary, and subsequently the Trinity:

The Messiah, Jesus Son of Mary,
Was only the messenger of God
And his word that he committed to Mary
And a spirit from him.
So believe in God and his messengers,
And say not "Three." (4:169)

O Jesus son of Mary,
Did'st thou say unto men
"Take me and my mother as gods
Apart from God?" (5:116)

The Messiah, son of Mary, was only a Messenger;
Messengers before him passed away;
His mother was just a woman;
They both ate food. (5:79)

THE PRIMACY OF THE QUR'AN

In 610 CE Muhammad was meditating in a cave on Mount Hira when Gabriel instructed him to recite three times. This was the beginning of revelations from Allah that came intermittently over the next twenty-three years. By 650 CE the Qur'an came together by compilation as the canonized holy text of Islam. Despite its obvious differences with other faith books, the Qur'an is the authoritative text of Islam and, in the view of Muslims, the final restoration of Allah's perfect message. Islam teaches that prior messengers provided Allah's revelations for humankind, but their messages were subsequently corrupted through translation or abuse. Caner and Caner write, "Islam teaches that the Qur'an is an exact word-for-word copy of God's final revelation, words inscribed on tablets that have always existed in heaven" (83). Thus, Muhammad's recitations provided the final opportunity for all humankind to reunite with Allah's purposes for creation. Ajiola adds, "It is on account of these special features of the Qur'an that all the people of the world have been directed to have faith in it, to give up all other books and to follow it alone, because it contains all that is essential for living in accordance with God's pleasure" (96). In many ways that would be foreign to the Western Christian mind, the Qur'an defines Islam. To the level of ink and stitching, the Qur'an is to be revered and followed in the pursuit of Islamic righteousness.

CHAPTER FIVE

Beliefs and Practices

At the heart of Islam is *tawhid*, the oneness of God. Another Arabic name for Allah is *al-Wahid* (the One), which illustrates the absoluteness of God. This singleness of thought is crucial to the act of being truly Muslim. *Islam* means "surrender" or "submission," although not in passive ways as those words suggest. Rather, this surrender is

> an engaged response to God. Like Judaism, Islam is a religion of orthopraxy (right conduct). By comparison, many Christians believe that all the great conduct in the world will not save a person; what is important is orthodoxy (right belief). Belief in Jesus as the Christ is at the heart of salvation. Muslims and Jews, to be sure, also have an understanding of what is right belief, but they are more concerned with performance of actions. (Hussain, 90–91)

The fact that Muslims have "Ninety-nine Wonderful Names" for Allah is another testament to the intense focus in Islam on "knowing" Allah. Muslims teach that Allah has seven unique qualities that help in understanding his magnitude.

• Life
• Hearing
• Knowledge
• Seeing
• Power
• Speech
• Will

David Brown, in *A Guide to Religions*, portrays the classic seven attributes of Allah this way:

> God lives eternally, without beginning or ending. He lives independently of the universe.
> God knows all things, past, present and future.
> God can do all things.
> All things exist as they are by the will of God.
> God hears all sounds; yet He has no ears as men have.
> God sees all things (even the steps of a black ant on a black stone on a dark night!); yet he has no eye as men have.
> God communicates with men. (207–208)

Each of these attributes are eternal, as is Allah, but they in no way assign him to the level or status of humankind. Allah does not have "hearing," but is *the* "Hearing." This means a person will never truly hear, see, speak, etc., outside of knowing Allah. Thus, Islam is a prescriptive religion that details ways in which to act first and believe second. For the Muslim, acts will always be superior to beliefs or dogma.

BECOMING MUSLIM

La ilaha illah wa Muhammadur rasul al-Lah: "There is no God but Allah, and Muhammad is the messenger of God." You have just read the *Shahadah*, the confession that bears witness to the Muslim faith. When individuals make this declaration and truly believe it in their hearts, they are "born anew" into life as a Muslim. The *Shahadah* is the first pillar of Islam. Islam has five pillars that are integral to life as a Muslim: "the Messenger of God said, 'Islam is built on five pillars (things): the testimony (There is no god but God and that Muhammad is the messenger of God); the performance of prayer; giving alms; the pilgrimage; and the fast of Ramadan'" (Lunde, 33). Listed succinctly, the five pillars are as follows:

1. The Creed (*Shahadah*): "There is no God but Allah, and Muhammad is his prophet."
2. Ritual Prayer (*Salat*): Five times per day—sunrise, noon, mid-afternoon, sunset, night.
3. Almsgiving (*Zakat*): Two-and-one-half percent to be given to the needy.
4. Fasting (*Sawm*): During Ramadan
5. Pilgrimage (*Hajj*): Once-in-life (if possible) trip to Mecca.

The *Shahadah*

The *Shahadah* is the equivalent of the Christian profession of faith and the Hebrew Shema. In effect, the *Shahadah* is the creed or statement of faith that best defines Islam. It means "to bear witness or testify" to the call in Islam to "remember Allah." Muhammad's initial message was to reconnect with the One True God of Abraham and Jesus and to disavow the false gods of Arabia. The *Shahadah* is the statement that accomplishes this religious and spiritual surrender to the reality of but one God. Conversion occurs when the *Shahadah* is recited with sincerity in front of Muslim witnesses. Devout Muslims repeat this foundational statement of faith daily to reaffirm their commitment to Allah.

The Prayers

The prayers of Muslims are to be undertaken five times per day (Shi'a combine two of the mandatory times and pray only three times), always facing Mecca. The first prayer must start at sunrise, the second when the sun is at its peak (noon), the third in the afternoon, the fourth at sundown, and the final prayer before going to bed. In adhering to this rigid schedule, Muslims place themselves in a state of constantly "remembering" Allah. These prayers have prescribed postures that reinforce attitudes of submission, primarily by prostration. A ritual cleansing is also mandated for each session of prayer. Muslims follow a ritual of purity that involves the washing of hands, face (including mouth and nostrils), arms, and feet. Women are required to wear head coverings, and both men and women are required to dress modestly. Muslim men are required to pray in the mosque on Friday, although this is optional for women. Men and women are separated in the mosque, as it is seen as improper for a man to witness a woman bent in prostration. The separation of men and women in the mosque has not always been in force. During the early Medinan period men and women participated equally in worship and prayer in the mosque. It was not until later that segregation became the norm. Galwash cites a spurious Hadith for the formal separation: "Muhammad stated that women pray better at home than in the mosque, and best of all in their own closets" (155–56).

Almsgiving

Almsgiving is required of all Muslims in order to assist the poor. The exact amount is determined by calculating a percentage of one's possessions, capital, and income. It is routinely taught that the *zakat* is two-and-one-half percent of one's worth on an annual basis. Wealth is seen as a blessing from Allah, and providing for the needy is seen as a natural response to one's personal blessing. Additional acts of charity are also encouraged and are considered a "loan to Allah" (2:245). These "extra-credit" acts can entail things as prolific as feeding the hungry to those as benign as smiling at one's neighbor.

Fasting

Fasting is required of Muslims during the annual Ramadan observance. The Muslim religious calendar is lunar, with each month extending from new moon to new moon, averaging 29 to 30 days in each cycle. This makes one year approximately 354 days, or 11 days shorter than the solar calendar. Jews also use a lunar calendar but synchronize their calendar by adding a periodic leap year. Islam forbids such synchronization, thus each annual festival or commemoration in Islam falls some 11 days earlier than in the previous year. This focus on a precise calendar is an example of the attention given to Ramadan by Muslims. Ramadan (the term for both the month and the observance) is the ninth month of the Muslim calendar and is easily the most important event in Islam. Adults are required to fast during daylight hours (women who are pregnant, nursing, or menstruating are not required to fast). This means a complete abstention from eating, drinking, smoking, or sexual activity from sunrise to sunset. Muslims rise especially early to eat a small meal and then declare their spiritual intention to fast for the remainder of daylight. The fast is broken each night after sunset with a ritual meal (*iftar*) and is normally followed by the evening prayer. Ramadan is seen as a demonstration of surrender and submission to Allah through the sacrifice of normal activities. The goal is to make oneself more aware of Allah through willpower and self-sacrifice.

Pilgrimage

The pilgrimage to Mecca is expected of each Muslim at least once in life. The *hajj* is to be undertaken during the twelfth month of the Muslim year by those who are able (physically or financially). Mecca is the "Holy City" of Islam and is revered as the place where Abraham was willing to sacrifice Ishmail. Mecca is also considered the site where Abraham and Ishmail rebuilt the *Kaa'bah* for the worship of Allah. The machinations of the actual pilgrimage (described in Sura 22:26-29) are long and complex.

Upon arrival in Mecca, "pilgrims" dress in a white garment to equalize all participants. They first walk counterclockwise around the *Kaa'bah* to symbolize the worship of one God, then run between the two hills of Safa and Marwa commemorating Allah's provision of water for Hagar and Ishmail. On the eighth day the pilgrims travel to the plain of Arafat, where they stand from noon to sunset praying and seeking mercy from Allah. This is done to emulate the Day of Judgment when all people will be resurrected and will stand before Allah for judgment. The plain of Arafat is spiritually significant for Muslims as it is where Muhammad delivered his final sermon and where he received his final revelation. The pilgrims next stop at Mina and throw pebbles at erected pillars representing Satan, sacrifice an animal to emulate Abraham's sacrifice of a ram, and then cut their hair (from one lock to the shaving of the head). The final act is again to walk around the *Kaa'bah* and finish the pilgrimage. Approximately two million Muslims travel to Mecca annually for the *hajj* experience.

SIX ARTICLES OF FAITH

Next in order of importance for Muslims are the six articles of faith. Islamic scholars and jurists cite these six beliefs as the intersection between orthopraxis (right practice) and orthodoxy (right belief). As previously stated, Islam differs from Christianity at the point of action over belief. The Christian primarily believes; the Muslim primarily acts. However, actions must be based on a specific, foundational belief structure, which is indicated by the six articles of faith.

1. Belief in Allah alone
2. Belief in angels, *jinn*, and Satan
3. Belief in the holy books
4. Belief in the Day of Reckoning
5. Belief in the Prophets
6. Belief in Predestination

Allah

Beyond the *Shahadah*, there is no creed required for one to be considered a Muslim. All an individual must do to convert to Islam is to recite the *Shahadah* in the presence of Muslim witnesses: "There is no God but God, and Muhammad is his prophet." This simple statement, or profession of faith, is not only the foundation of all articles of faith, but it is Islamic theology encapsulated. The *tawhid*, or oneness of God, is more than simple monotheism. "When Muslims cry Allahu Akbar! (literally, 'God is greater!'), what they mean is not God is greater than this or that, but that God is simply greater" (Aslan, 150). To understand Islam is first to understand this foundational theological implication:

> The orthodox Muslim conception of God may be summed up as follows: God is one; He has no partners; Singular without any like Him; Uniform, having no contrary; Separate, having no equal;

Ancient, having no first; Ever-existing, without termination; Perpetual and constant, with neither interruption nor ending; Ever qualified with the attributes of supreme greatness; nor is He bound to be determined by lapses of ages or times. He is both the Alpha and the Omega, the Manifest and the Hidden, He is real. (Galwash, 139)

Each of Allah's ninety-nine names points to his being before, above, and beyond all things, and it is to this level of omnipotence that Islam ascribes. The key for Muslims is to "remember" Allah in all the ways he is portrayed. This is done primarily through adherence to the five pillars.

Angels

Muslim theology teaches that three uncreated entities exist: (a) Allah; (b) the "Mother of the Book"; and (c) angels who surround the throne upon which Allah is seated in the Seventh Heaven. Muslims believe that angels are pure, sexless beings who attend to Allah, often as messengers who fight alongside believers against unbelievers. Angels also serve as "guardians" of Muslims. Certain angels escort the dead to Hell, and others mediate on behalf of humankind. It is also believed that each person has two accompanying angels that serve as "recorders." These tandem angels activate each person's conscience and take note of every good and bad deed for use on Judgment Day.

> As for those who say: "Our Lord is God," and take the straight path to Him, the angels will descend to them, saying: "Have no fear, and do not grieve. Rejoice in the Paradise you have been promised. We are your guardians in this world and in the world to come." (Sura 41:30-31)

Angels play a large role in day-to-day Muslim life. Many of the same angels that play significant roles in the Bible, namely Gabriel and Michael, are also involved in the Qur'an. The Qur'an depicts the level of importance placed on these two angels by Allah:

Say (O Muhammad to mankind): Who is an enemy to Gabriel! For he it is who hath revealed this scripture to thy heart by Allah's leave, confirming that which was (revealed) before it, and a guidance and glad tidings to believers; who is an enemy to Allah and His angels and His messengers, and Gabriel and Michael! Then, lo! Allah (Himself) is an enemy to the disbelievers. (Sura 2:97-98)

Satan

The Qur'an shares with the Bible the teaching of a fallen angel or Satan, also called *Iblis*. In the Qur'anic account Satan was an angel who was present at the creation of Adam, the first man. All angels were commanded to bow before the newly created person and worship him. Satan refused:

"Satan," said He, "why do you not bow to him whom my own hands have made? Are you too proud, or do you deem yourself superior?" Satan replied, "I am nobler than he. You created me from fire, but him from clay." (Sura 38:77)

Islamic teaching is split on whether Satan was a fallen angel or a *jinn*. Arabs believed *jinn* to be invisible creatures born of smokeless fire. The Qur'an teaches that Allah created these mystical beings: "We created man from sounding clay, from mud molded into shape; and the *Jinn* race, We had Created before, from the fire of a scorching wind" (Sura 15:26-27). Muslims see the *jinn* as creatures of great power and intelligence who possess abilities for both good and evil. They reportedly take on various forms and have been implicated in the possession of unsuspecting souls. In the West the *jinn* are commonly caricatured, known as genies, and are portrayed as residing mostly in magic bottles and having the power to grant wishes.

Holy Books

Muslims acknowledge four holy books: the Qur'an and three portions of the Bible: the Pentateuch or Law of Moses, the Psalms of David, and the Gospel of Jesus.

O believers, believe in God and His Messenger and the Book He
has sent down on His Messenger and the Book which He sent down
before. Whoso disbelieves in God and His angels and His Books,
and His Messengers, and the Last Day, has surely gone astray into
far error. (Sura 4:13)

Islam acknowledges the "People of the Book," Christians and
Jews, but almost simultaneously dismisses the actual relevance of the
Bible. It is believed that God provided the earlier scriptures as revelation to humankind, but over time they became corrupted and were
rendered futile. These former revelations came to be "beyond repair"
and were replaced by the Qur'an, the final revelation. The Qur'an
consistently contradicts the Bible, especially in regard to the status and
role of Jesus. Nevertheless, it is incumbent upon Muslims to regard
the *original* Hebrew and Christian scriptures as holy and originating
from Allah. Christine Huda Dodge expresses the unique Muslim position on earlier holy writings: "Islam's position on the Bible is that the
book in circulation today does not accurately reflect the teachings of
Jesus or the beliefs of his early followers. While some passages may
seem to correspond with Islamic teaching, Muslims find most of the
book, and certainly the modern translations and interpretations, to be
corrupted" (69).

Day of Reckoning

Muslims believe in a coming time of judgment when Allah will bring
forth the scales of justice and all people will be called into account. In
the Qur'an there are suras dealing specifically with resurrection, judgment, Paradise, and the realities of Hell. Upon death the body returns
to the dust while the soul slips into an unconscious state. At the time
of judgment Allah will call forth all who are alive and those already
dead and begin the process of assigning eternal position. During this
protracted time, people will seek redress against tormentors who will
be made to surrender a portion of their good works to the victims. It
will also be a time when people will seek intercession from their
prophets, although none will be bestowed. After final judgment is
passed down, each person will walk over a narrow bridge (Jahannam)

to their respective destinations. The bridge is constructed in such a way that the favored will navigate with ease and enter Paradise, while the evil will stumble and fall off into Hell.

Before the end of time, Muslims believe that the *Mahdi* will return to guide Islam through great opposition. Iranian academic Seyyed Nasr writes,

> The end of human history will be marked by the advent of the coming of a person named the Mahdi, who will destroy oppression, defeat the enemies of religion, and reestablish peace and justice on earth. Sunnis believe the Mahdi to be a member of the tribe of the Prophet bearing the name of Muhammad while the Shiites identify him with the Twelfth Imam. Both branches believe that the rule of the Mahdi will be followed by the return of Christ to Jerusalem, which will bring humanity to a close and lead to the Day of Judgment. (74)

It should be noted that Islam does not view Jesus' final role as bringing about salvation. Rather, he will be a symbol of the oneness of Allah, which is the foundational belief of Islam. It is taught that Jesus will die after his final work is accomplished and that he will be buried near Muhammad.

The final destination of humankind will be determined on the Day of Reckoning. Those found righteous will be allowed into Paradise, and those found unrighteous will be sent to Hell. Paradise in Islam differs greatly from the Heaven of Christianity. In the latter, the existence will be purely spiritual and entirely non-earthly. Muslims teach that Paradise will be filled with sensual delights and culinary treats. Paradise will provide fine clothes made of silk, free-flowing drink, fountains of honey, and groves of exotic fruit. Paradise will also offer *houris*, beautiful virgins who will attend to the needs of men: ". . . and we shall espouse them to wide-eyed *houris* . . . perfectly we formed them, perfect, and we made them spotless virgins, chastely amorous. . ." (Sura 44; Sura 56).

Muslims believe Hell has seven entrances and seven levels. Hell will be a place of torment commensurate to the life led on earth. It is described as the abode of the unrepentant and the idolater who will wear clothes of pitch and have only boiling water and pus to drink. A small portion of Muslims believe Hell to be a place of refinement and purification and think that ultimately everyone will be granted entrance into Paradise. The majority, however, view Hell as the final and eternal home of the unrighteous.

Prophets

Islam teaches that Allah reveals his will to humankind through prophets. This practice was established from the earliest times as Adam, after his sin, repented and became the prophet to the first created peoples. Despite its seemingly revisionist logic, Muslims esteem Adam as the first prophet despite Abraham often being credited with being the first Muslim. The list of prophets is long, with 124,000 referred to in the holy writings, requiring that a delineation be made between prophets and messengers. Messengers are prophets sent to a specific people to deliver a specific message. Islamic tradition lists the number of messengers as approximately 300. Beyond the prophetic messenger are those who are given an actual text to present to the people. That number is but five, and they are Abraham, Moses, David, Jesus, and Muhammad. Noah is considered by some to be among the elite prophets as he was reportedly given laws concerning marriage and diet to pass on to the people.

Muslims revere Jesus as the second most important prophet, and to that end he is mentioned by name ninety-seven times in the Qur'an. He is referred to by such titles as "Messiah" and "spirit of God," and is portrayed as performing miracles as a child and having a virgin birth. Despite the lofty status of Jesus in Islam, he is, in the end, seen only as a major messenger: "The Messiah, the son of Mary, was no more than an apostle: other apostles passed away before him. His mother was a saintly woman. They both ate earthly food" (Sura 5:75).

Muhammad is seen as the final messenger, the "Seal of the Prophets," and as "Witness" and "Warner." Braswell writes,

> His message was the same as all other major prophets before him, including the Torah and the Gospel of Jesus. He superseded all pre-

vious prophets, messengers and revelations. However, since their messages before Muhammad have been either lost or corrupted, Muhammad brings the final and perfect message in the Qur'an. He is the last prophet. (23)

Predestination and Free Will

Muslims teach the Divine Decree, the doctrine that all things have been decided by Allah and, consequently, all things come from him. This doctrine is one of "determinism" and is closely associated with the Christian view of predestination. In both religions, questions abound when considering the accompanying question of human free choice. If God has already ordained all events, are people really free to choose? C. T. R. Hewer writes,

> One of the most perplexing issues facing all monotheistic religions is how to make humans responsible for . . . [their] own actions while maintaining the absolute power of God. Put another way, is it possible for a person to hold the power of self-choice and for God to remain Omnipotent? A follow-up question . . . pertains to the holiness of God. If God is supremely holy, how could God assign evil acts? If God both knew the wicked things someone would do and wrote that into the person's destiny, does that make God evil and wicked? (81)

These questions have split Muslim scholars and jurists for centuries. One group holds that humans enjoy complete free will and thus deserve the consequences of their individual actions. Other groups teach a doctrine of predestination that suggests people naturally act out their assigned parts. The latter is the majority belief in Islam and assigns Allah as author of a script from which humans cannot veer in life. This absolute and concrete doctrine makes it easy to define the omnipotence of Allah: "the One who creates what He wills." "God created you and created what you make" (Sura 37:96). A. J. Wensinck writes, "Before Creation God decreed and wrote down the exact course of events for his creation, with practical implications that are lucidly summed up in the words of an early creed: 'What reaches you could not possibly have missed you; and that what misses you could not possibly have reached you'" (103). A Muslim tradition also teaches that on the forty-second day, an embryo is assigned an exact date of death.

All deterministic religions are forced from within to confront the corresponding questions of human activity and choice. Islam was forced to deal with this issue in the tenth century by the Mu'tazilite sect that formed over this primary question:

> The Mu'tazilites taught that the Qur'an declares that humans will be rewarded or punished according to their own deeds. If one's deeds are not one's own, God would be unjust to punish or reward the individual. Belief in the justice of God requires a corresponding belief in human freedom, for if humans are not free, God is not just. (Brown, 138)

The Mu'tazilites were influential for only a short period of time, and the prevailing doctrine remains in place that Allah has mandated life for the individual Muslim. Rather than continue the debate and possibly interfere with the core focus on Allah's oneness, the Muslim adage of "Don't ask why" was employed. Since Islam was founded on the unity and oneness of "the God" (al-Lah), each Muslim is taught to make a sincere effort to do his or her best in every situation. No Muslim is allowed to resign effectively from life or give in to blind fate. Since no individuals can truly know their own destiny, they must strive to live the Muslim principles and to emulate Muhammad: "Belief in the Divine decree is thus a statement of belief in the meaningfulness and purposefulness of all that is, an essential part of the Muslim's sense of total trust, dependence and submission in relation to his Creator" (Haneef, 40).

COMMANDMENTS

Islam does not have a precise list of commandments as the Hebrews do, but Muslims are expected to live out in daily life the major commands found within the Qur'an, Hadith, and the Sunnah. Caesar E.

Farah has compiled the ten most applicable commandments asked of each Muslim:

1. Acknowledge there is no god whatsoever but Allah.
2. Honor and respect parents.
3. Respect the rights of others.
4. Be generous but never squander money.
5. Avoid killing except for justifiable cause.
6. Do not commit adultery.
7. Safeguard the possessions of orphans.
8. Deal justly and equitably.
9. Be pure of mind and heart.
10. Be humble and unpretentious.

HEAVEN AND HELL

The afterlife is gravely important to Muslims. Some 25 percent of the Qur'an is dedicated to statements related to the eternal condition—specifically, judgment, Paradise, and Hell. Muslim teaching states that the decisions of this life will determine the terms of the life to follow. Paradise is reserved for the righteous, and Hell will be the abode of the unrighteous. Both possible destinations are described in graphic and vivid detail in the Qur'an and Hadith:

> Then those whose balance of good deeds is heavy will attain salvation, but those whose balance is light will have lost their souls and abide in Hell forever. (Sura 23:102-103)

> Hell will lie in ambush, a home for the transgressors. There they shall abide long ages; there they shall taste neither refreshment nor any drink save boiling water and decaying filth, a fitting recompense. (Sura 78:21)

> Those who have denied the Book and the message We sent through Our apostles shall realize the truth hereafter: when, with chains and shackles around their necks, they shall be dragged through scalding water and burnt in the fire of Hell. (Sura 40:71)

They that deny our revelations We will burn in fire. No sooner will their skins be consumed, We shall give them other skins, so that they may truly taste the scourge. God is mighty and wise. (Sura 4:56)

God will deliver them from the evil of that day, and make their faces shine with joy. He will reward them for their steadfastness with Paradise and robes of silk. Reclining there upon soft couches, they shall feel neither the scorching heat nor the biting cold. Trees will spread their shade around them, and fruits will hang in clusters over them. (Sura 76:12)

. . . the true servants of God shall be well provided for, feasting on fruit, and honored in the gardens of delight. Reclining face to face upon soft couches, they shall be served with a goblet filled at a gushing fountain, white, and delicious to those who drink it. It will neither dull their senses nor befuddle them. They shall sit with bashful, dark-eyed virgins, as chaste as the sheltered eggs of ostriches. (Sura 37:41-49)

But in fair gardens the righteous shall dwell in bliss, rejoicing in what their Lord will give them. Their Lord will shield them from the scourge of Hell. He will say, "Eat and drink to your hearts' content." This is the reward of your labors. They shall recline on couches arranged in rows. To dark-eyed houris We shall wed them. Fruits We shall give them, and such meats as they desire. They will pass from hand to hand a cup inspiring no idle talk, no sinful urge; and there shall wait on them young boys of their own, as fair as virgin pearls. (Sura 52:17-24)

The Muslim afterlife of Hell is depicted in graphic, even gory detail in the authorized texts: "The Qur'an describes Hell as a roasting place, as pus, as boiling water. Vivid torture is depicted with boiling brains and molten lead poured into ears. It is a burning and odious place" (Braswell, 30). Muslim Hell is seen as the destination for those who did not adequately live as proper Muslims. A negative balance of good works will result in eternal punishment for the Muslim. Islam is a religion of judgment, not mercy. This dogma is not good news for those deemed as guilty, but is extremely positive for the righteous.

In Islam, Paradise is basically the exact opposite of Hell. Rather than drink pus and boiling water, the righteous will bask in all things enjoyable and "un-desert-like" for all of eternity:

> Heaven, then, is the antithesis of hell as gardens replace fire and shade replaces roasting. Since Allah is satisfied with the righteous, he gives them eternal security, fruit and drink, and chaste women! Men will sit on raised couches drinking new wine and looking at beautiful virgins. (Caner and Caner, 149)

A close reading of the Qur'an and Hadith clearly show that most references to Paradise feature perks that would not have been available in the desert landscape of Arabia. Cold milk would have been enticing to the average seventh-century Arab. With the prohibition of alcohol in Islam, free-flowing wine would also attract great attention. Paradise also seems to feature sensual delights that are patently male-dominated. The Qur'anic description of *houris*, dark-eyed, young, and chaste beauties, is now infamous; but is it accurate? Do men actually spend time with specially created perfect females in Paradise, and if so, what do Muslim women experience in the afterlife?

There is great debate over these questions in Muslim theology, and no clear consensus exists. It is widely taught that righteous Muslim women will also enter into Paradise. There are no Qur'anic verses that state otherwise, but neither are there any that feature women exclusively. In most cases the inclusive, plural nouns "servants" or "believers" are employed, signifying both genders. There seems to be virtually no doubt that both men and women are eligible for Paradise. The exact role and status of women in Paradise is the larger question. A follow-up query would focus on the nature of Paradise: Is it sensual or is it spiritual?

Once again, there is no consensus among Muslim scholars and specialists. Braswell sees the environment as being literal (to the Qur'an) and highly sensual:

Paradise offers both sensual and sexual delights. For men there are beautiful virgins (houris). There are various quarters in heaven to which one may aspire. In some traditions, wives are kept in separate quarters where their husbands may discreetly visit them. Married men are described as having new wives who are sensual, charming, and eternally youthful. (30)

Parshall describes the *houris* as "special creatures of God who exist for the eternal enjoyment of Muslim men. These creatures will remain eternally young and beautiful." He goes on to say that there are no references to women having husbands or even a husband (146).

Richard Henry Drummond takes this debate to a new level with his views:

In the gardens of green there will also be houris available for believers. These maidens are always spoken of as good and comely, as modestly restraining their glances (an ancient ideal). And God will wed these "wide-eyed houris to believers." It would seem that polygamy will prevail in Paradise as on earth, apparently without limitation to the earthly permitted number of four wives. (90–91)

If this view is correct, Paradise will be an experience of indulging in all the activities that were prohibited during the earthly, human experience.

Of course, the question of sensuality versus spirituality in Paradise is also one with diametrically differing opinions. The Qur'an and Hadith contain conflicting statements: *houris* being intended for the pleasure of men and there being no sexuality permitted in Paradise. Christine Huda Dodge believes the word *houri* is more "companion" than partner, and that no sexual connotation exists (158). John Esposito agrees: "The Qur'an makes no reference to a sexual role for the *houris.* However, many Qur'anic commentators and most Muslims understand *houris* as virgins only in the sense of pure or purified souls" (29). Again, this is a debate that will continue as the texts of Islam do not allow for it to be settled with certainty. However, there can be no middle ground in this debate. Paradise will be sensual, or entirely spiritual, and women will be virtually invisible, or they will be equal with men for all eternity.

Muslims teach that whether one is destined for Paradise or Hell, the arrival time is long after death. There is no concept of instant gratification in Islam pertaining to Paradise. Islam teaches that the Angel of Death arrives at the moment of death to remove the soul of the dying person. Special angels then escort the soul to the gates of Paradise. At that point the soul learns where it will spend eternity. The angels then escort the soul back to the earth to await the Day of Judgment.

CHAPTER SIX

Islamic Law

SHARI'A

In Islam there are no lines drawn between the secular and spiritual life of the individual Muslim. Guidelines, instructions, and examples are drawn from the Qur'an, Sunnah, and Hadith for almost every aspect of daily life. Prayer, legal questions, gender roles, dietary specifications, dress codes, and much more are provided within the *Shari'a*. For things not expressly covered by the texts of Islam and thus not evident in the eighth century, the texts are supplemented by consensus and analogies. Islam has ruled on areas such as abortion, birth control, and organ donation by using consensus and analogies. When one considers how expansive *Shari'a* is to Islamic life, it is easy to agree with Farah's assertion that "*Shari'a* is Islam's constitution" (160). Nasr adds, "The Shari'a, or Divine Law of Islam, not only is central to the religion, but also constitutes Islam itself in its ritual, legal, ethical, and social aspects. . . . Shari'a contains the concrete embodiment of the Will of God" (75).

Shari'a comes from the Arabic root meaning "road." *Shari'a* is thus the road or path that men and women must follow in life. The road of Islam would also include all aspects of government, as there is no line drawn between mosque and state. The inherent completeness of this law-to-life system could be both cumbersome and confusing if not for the categorical divisions in place. *Shari'a* divides all human actions into seven broad categories to ensure understanding, clarification, and application:

1. *Fard*: Those actions that are obligatory under law.
2. *Wajib*: Actions that are obligatory but not expressly mentioned in the primary sources of law.
3. *Mustahabb*: Actions that are not obligatory but are recommended.
4. *Muhab*: Neutral or permitted acts.
5. *Makruh*: Actions that are not forbidden but discouraged.
6. *Haram*: Actions that are absolutely forbidden.
7. *Halal*: That which is permitted.

Aslan writes, "These seven categories are designed to demonstrate Islam's overarching concern with not only forbidding vice, but also actively promoting virtue" (162). These categories also demonstrate the importance of "works" in Islam. The seven areas of Islamic law are purely functional and do not focus on spirituality. They represent the essence of what should and should not be done in the practice of Islam. Further, they create a "how-to" guide for the function of all that is required to honor Allah.

In early Islam there were no lines drawn to separate social, political, personal, or religious aspects of life. In fact, no line between mosque and state has ever existed in orthodox Islam. In many moderate societies where *Shari'a* has given way to secular codes of law and government, fundamentalist groups have attempted to force comprehensive Islamic law back into the social equation. Peter Cotterell explains that the legal, not theological, aspects of Islam are at the heart of Islamic extremism:

> The insistence that a Muslim government must introduce *Shari'a* law, so that Muslim people may live as they should, is at the heart of the rise of the radical Islamist movement in Islam. Radicalism in Islam is quite different from any equivalent in Christianity. It is not a matter of adherence to fundamental theological beliefs, but a demand for the addition of those undisputed beliefs into a Qur'an-based civil and criminal code of law. (46)

Shari'a covers virtually all major offenses that occur within a society. There are specific punishments for crimes such as murder, assault, theft, and adultery, as well as for acts that would not be considered criminal in most cultures. The penalties for murder can be either execution or monetary compensation to the victim's family. For an intentional injury, an injury equal to the one caused or monetary compensation to the victim is required. Theft is punished by cutting off one hand, unless the individual stole out of true need and necessity. Fornication brings flogging for both parties, and the penalty for adultery is stoning to death for both the man and woman. Homosexual acts are punished by the execution of both partners, while alcohol consumption leads to flogging.

The degree that *Shari'a* is applied in today's world varies greatly from region to region. A complete embrace of classic Islamic law would be to accept a legal system based primarily on the Qur'an and rooted in seventh-century desert Arabia. To say that punishments are dated, especially by Western standards, would be grand understatement. *Shari'a* is difficult to apply to a naturally secular society. For this reason, the numbers of purely Shari'a-based states have been drastically reduced. Saudia Arabia has at its base the *Shari'a* system. In the late 1970s Iran re-implemented *Shari'a* after the shah was deposed and the ayatollah assumed control. Turkey and Egypt are modern examples of countries that have predominant Muslim populations but opt for secular structures for law and government. However, the uniqueness and all-encompassing nature of *Shari'a* allows for Muslims to apply it to their individual lives regardless of locale. While it is required that an authorized court determine guilt, the forms of punishment are badly dated. This reality has led moderate Islamic societies either to meld *Shari'a* into secular codes or to do away with it altogether.

ETHICS AND VALUES

Muslims are taught to participate in certain prescribed acts and to avoid other specific ones. These *halal*, or permitted, and *haram*, or forbidden, acts define the values and ethics of prescribed Islamic practices. It would be easy to confuse *halal* and *haram* with Hebrew concepts of kosher or non-kosher, but Islam goes well beyond food and beverage stipulations. Virtually all of life is prescribed for the

Muslim and consequently falls into the *halal* or *haram* categories. Ruqaiyyah Waris Maqsood lists the *halal* and *haram* values of Islam. The following acts are encouraged in Islam:

Faith	Humility
Justice	Tolerance
Forgiveness	Modesty
Compassion	Chastity
Mercy	Patience
Sincerity	Responsibility
Truth	Courage
Generosity	

He also lists those things that must be avoided in life:

Hypocrisy	Envy
Cheating	Anger
Backbiting	Divisiveness
Suspicion	Excess
Lying	Extremism
Pride	

The Islamic duties of values and ethics may be summarized by these verses from the Qur'an and Hadith:

Goodness and Evil cannot be equal. Repay evil with what is better, then he who was your enemy will become your intimate friend. (Sura 41:34)

You shall not enter Paradise until you have faith, and you cannot have faith until you love one another. Have compassion on those you can see, and He Whom you cannot see will have compassion on you. (Hadith)

USURY

Islamic law does not accept the concept of a Western economic system, as the practice of charging interest is forbidden in the Qur'an. Usury (*riba*) or levying interest amounts on loans, has been looked down upon since the time of Muhammad. Sura 2:275 reads, "Those who devour usury will not stand except as stands one whom the Evil One by his touch hath driven to madness. That is because they say: 'Trade is like usury.' But Allah hath not permitted trade and forbidden usury." The common teaching behind this prohibition is twofold: First, in a society with zero inflation, no charges on loaned money or goods are necessary. Second, "prohibiting usury is clearly associated in the Qur'an with charity, for inasmuch as charity is the broad basis of human sympathy, usury annihilates all sympathetic affections" (Ali, 530).

FOOD AND DRINK

Muslims are provided guidelines for the consumption of food and drink. Islam prohibits certain foods in the interest of health and cleanliness, while promoting others for many of the same reasons. All forbidden foods are considered *haram*, all others are *halal* and may be enjoyed by all Muslims. It should be noted that both Jews and Muslims are allowed to break the dietary restrictions if survival depends on doing so.

Islam prohibits the eating of pork and the ingestion of blood. Slaughtered animals must be killed in a quick and merciful manner, and any animal that dies a natural death is forbidden as food. Predatory animals are forbidden, as well as animals slaughtered in the name of a false god. Hunting for sport is not permitted. Islam permits the consumption of all seafood. Smoking is pervasive in most Muslim cultures due to the relatively late discovery of the life-threatening health dangers involved. No alteration to *Shari'a* law has been undertaken to counter this dangerous life practice.

Alcohol and other intoxicants are forbidden in all three Muslim texts. In fact, various types of wine were declared *haram* early in the

Meccan period. Bukhari's Hadith text states, "prohibited wine was made of five things, grapes, dates, wheat, barley and honey" (74:4). In the early days in Medina, Muhammad stated, "They ask thee about intoxicants and games of chance. Say: In both of them is great sin and some advantage for men, and their sin is greater than their advantage" (2:219). It is obvious that some Medinan Muslims did not pay attention, as a later sura addressed the issue of men coming to the mosque intoxicated: "O you who believe, Go not near prayer when you are intoxicated until you know what you say" (4:43). Many years later the use of reason and analogy was undertaken to determine if the new beverage of beer was acceptable: "As long as fuqqa, a beverage made of barley, does not intoxicate there is no harm" (Bukhari's Hadith, 74:8). Drugs and herbs that led to intoxication were also forbidden for Muslims.

It was also in the Medinan period that games of chance and other sundry habits became problematic in Islam. Muhammad dealt with the issue in this manner: "O you who believe, intoxicants and games of chance and sacrificing to stones and dividing by arrows are only an uncleanness, the devil's work; so shun it that you may succeed" (5:90).

CLOTHING

Islam prohibits the exploitation of both the male and female bodies. Modesty in dress is commanded for both genders and any forms of public nudity are expressly prohibited. While Maulana Muhammad Ali states that no limitations are placed upon the form or quality of clothing in either the Qur'an or Hadith (*Religion of Islam*, 547), the reality is that Muhammad did command the veil for women. Women did not wear veils in pre-Islamic Arabia, but they did so in virtually all neighboring countries. It is believed that Islam adopted this practice from the Syrian, Persian, and Byzantine cultures, which sheltered their women out of respect and honor. Ironically, Muhammad's direction for the veil was primarily focused upon the home and not the public fare. Due to the early Muslim home also being a place of business and thus heavily trafficked, women were asked to remain secluded beyond a curtain or veil. He later mentioned veils for the purpose of modesty in Sura 24:31: "Let them cast their veils over their bosoms, and not reveal their adornment save to their husbands." It was much later that these restrictions led to full-blown segregation in the mosque and women bearing all responsibility in not leading men to commit the sin of sexual temptation.

Hijab (or veiling) when leaving one's house indicates modesty in dress and behavior. A woman in *hijab* is a covered woman. Discussion only arises over the extent of the *hijab*, or cover. Muslim women do not wish to display their physical beauty in public. That is something reserved for their husbands, for whom they should make themselves as beautiful and attractive as possible (Maqsood, 235).

The proliferation of this issue led to many new clothing commands being placed upon Muslim women, all of which are still in place today in the most fundamentalist countries. The *hijab* literally means "barrier" and is the head covering worn by the majority of Muslim women. To many modern Muslim scholars the *hijab* is the maximum covering for the female required by either the Qur'an or Hadith. Other clothing requirements are in place, however, and they differ from society to society. The *chador* is a loose-fitting black cloak that covers the body, head, and hair, but not the face. It is the required outfit for females above age nine in Iran. The *burqa* is a heavier and larger version of the *chador* and conceals the entire figure. A mesh covering for the eyes is sewn into the headpiece. The Taliban enforced this mode of dress in Afghanistan, and it is also worn in parts of Pakistan, India, and on the Arabian Peninsula. The *abaya* is a loose black robe that covers a woman from head to toe and is worn in Saudia Arabia (Roraback, 38).

One important element that the Western observer often misunderstands is that the Muslim woman rarely views the *hijab* as being restrictive. Madeline Bunting spent time discussing clothing requirements with British Muslim women and reports,

> What they hotly deny is that veiling, and modesty in public, is a form of repression. It is not about shame of the female body, as western feminists sometimes insist, but about claiming privacy over their bodies. These women wonder how western women have

"reclaimed" their bodies, yet at the same time, allowed for more public expression of sexuality. In Islam it is about female modesty and not sexuality. (3)

Muslim law dictates that neither men nor women should dress provocatively and as a result lead another person into sin. For the most part, men have ignored these directions to a much greater degree than have women. Muslim men are required to dress modestly and never to excess. The particular area that men must never publicly exhibit extends from the navel to the knee. Men are commanded not to wear silk nor wear feminine clothes or accessories. Men are also prohibited from wearing tight or transparent clothes. In some Muslim societies men are required to wear head coverings, although this is not a requirement found in any of the texts of Islam.

The overriding expectation in orthodox Islam is that each person comport himself or herself in a manner that promotes virtue and guards against sensual temptation. For Muslims, this mindset of purity is to be the rationale for all clothing choices. It is also commanded that unrelated men and women are not to make eye-to-eye contact when they meet in public: "Lower your gaze and guard your modesty" (Sura 24:30-31). As Amir Hussain observes, "Islamic approaches to dress recognize the cross-gender sexual dynamic that exists between men and women—hence an emphasis on modesty" (149).

CHAPTER SEVEN

Women in Islam

Islam faces two great questions as it dominates the world's attention in the twenty-first century: Is Islam a peaceful religion, and does Islam provide women equality with men? The answer to both queries is simply yes and no. There is hardly a gray area in either debate, especially as relating to the role and status of women. Muhammad did improve the status, rights, and social position of women in and through early Islam. At some point, however, those equitable rights were corrupted and women were relegated to a level far below that of men in most areas of life. The remaining questions do not have to do with whether this occurred; rather, they focus on when it occurred and why.

In some cases the disparities between the sexes have to do with role and function. The Qur'an does display a spiritual equality where Allah sees men and women as equal, although females face many more regulations relating to Ramadan, mosque, *hajj*, and leadership. The roles of women in the first years were in stark contrast to those of men. Karen Armstrong writes,

> The Holy Book takes for granted, as indeed it had to in seventh century Arabia, that men lead the community, fight, hunt, preach and make law. Women raise children and tend to domestic duties. Women are equal before God and will be judged on the last day by the same standards as men. The Qur'an also belittles women and cites men's authority over them. (96)

The Qur'an is quite confusing on the status of women. Sura 16:97 reads, "We shall reward the steadfast according to their noblest deeds. Be they men or women, those that embrace the faith and do what is right We will surely grant a happy life." However, Sura 4:34 states, "Men have authority over women because they spend their wealth to maintain them. Good women are obedient. They guard their unseen parts because Allah has guarded them. As for those from whom you fear disobedience, admonish them and send them to bed apart and beat them."

Karen Armstrong is one of the leading Islamic specialists and is also known primarily as an apologist (advocate) for the religion. She provides valuable insight on this perplexing dichotomy, reporting that one of Muhammad's primary goals was to provide women with unprecedented status and opportunities. The Qur'an also gave women rights of inheritance and divorce centuries before Western women were accorded such status (Armstrong, 16). The reality seems, however, that what the Qur'an provides, the Qur'an sometimes takes away. Due to the process of abrogation, it is difficult to determine which verses were cancelled by later revelations. With the simplest marker being that verses found in the front of the Qur'an were actually spoken later, the first portions would be applicable to today's Islam. If this is the case, Islam changed its views on women during Muhammad's ministry.

> Women shall with justice have rights similar to those exercised against them, although men have a status above women. (Sura 2:228)

> Women are your fields; go then, into your fields whence you please. (2:223)

> Call in two male witnesses from among you, but if two men cannot be found, then one man and two women whom you judge fit to act as a witness; so that if either of them commit an error, the other will remember. (2:282)

Muhammad is also reported to have said that the majority of those who will inhabit Hell will be the poor and women. However, rather than focusing on the "unequal" equality of women in Islam, it should be noted that women did indeed fare better as Muslims than in the pagan Arabian religions. Before Islam, women were treated as little more than property that could be purchased, sold, or bartered. Women were blamed for all misfortune and were considered by many to be subhuman. The birth of a female child often brought mourning and shame. It was not uncommon for the infant girl to be buried alive to relieve the shame on the family. There is no doubt that Muhammad and Islam improved the status of women immensely. It may seem to be a shaky equality to the twenty-first-century Western observer, but it was an improvement of epic proportions for Arabia and for many of the countries early Islam ruled.

MARRIAGE

Muslims consider marriage to be the most important element of life beyond the *Shahadah*. Marriage, however, is not thought of as a mystical sacrament "made in heaven," but as a social contract that brings rights, responsibilities, roles, and obligations. If both partners adhere to the above elements and mutually respect each other, the union is deemed successful (Maqsood, 210). This doesn't mean Muslims do not see spiritual elements within the marriage process. It pays to remember that "life is Islam and Islam is life," thus every part of one's existence is religion. To this end, and respecting the Islamic view of Allah's oneness, Muslim marriage has the expectation of permanency.

There are an amazing number of rules concerning marriage in Islam. It seems bizarre there needed to be specific legislation prohibiting the following groups from entering into a marriage:

Stepmothers and stepsons; stepfathers and stepdaughters
Mothers and children; fathers and children
Sisters and brothers
Aunts and nephews; uncles and nieces
Grandparents and grandchildren

Mothers-in-law and sons-in-law; fathers-in-law and daughters-in-law (Dodge, 206)

In light of pre-Islamic Arabian customs and tribal practices, the above restrictions were necessary to preserve the family structure and to prevent incest. These dangers were drastically reduced in Islam, but much of the Islamic structure was created due to this type of desert tribal existence.

Dating practices are also different within a Muslim environment. In the West a couple can spend time together unchaperoned, especially after engagement. In a Muslim country a chaperone is required and little time is provided for a couple to be alone. Chastity is prescribed in Islam. The penalties for premarital sex are severe, and the female could lose all standing within the community if convicted.

The act of marriage is in the form of a covenant in the Qur'an. The covenant is entered into by the mutual consent of two parties in the presence of witnesses. The focus on mutual consent is in place to ensure that the female has actually agreed to the marriage. Most marriages in pre-Islamic Arabia were arranged, and the female had no choice in the matter. Muhammad did not do away with the practice; rather he provided the woman with an equal vote on the arrangement. Presently, arranged marriages take place mostly in the more conservative Muslim societies. Muhammad also instituted a wedding sermon into the previous Arabic structure, which remains a central element of the ceremony. Often the groom delivers the sermon and the bride is obligated to affirm his words. Islam demands a unique element in the marriage process called *walimah*. This is an Arabic word for "publicity" and is intended to announce the marriage to the larger population. The fear of "secret" marriages seems to be the focus here, and for this reason the *walimah* is often large and long. It is not uncommon for a *walimah* to last for three days.

Islam requires a dowry to be part of the marriage contract. The dowry is also known as the Nuptial Gift in modern Islam. In many non-Muslim cultures the bride's family provides the dowry, but it is the opposite in Islam. The man must provide a dowry to the woman, and if the marriage ends in divorce, she is allowed to keep the full gift.

Tradition states that the dowry must be paid by the time of consummation, or at a legally stated time thereafter. This would ensure that a man would not take advantage of a woman by marrying her, all the while keeping the dowry at bay with the intent of not delivering. It is also believed that the higher the dowry, the less likely the husband will be to invoke a divorce.

DIVORCE

Muhammad began his teaching in a society that was known for degrading women to the level of inexpensive property. Marriage was weighted heavily in the favor of the man and women had few, if any, rights. Muhammad made changes that allowed for women to have virtually equal rights within marriage. This did not extend to the termination of a marriage, however, as men could divorce by stating "I divorce you" three times in the presence of witnesses. Muhammad did teach that marriage was for life and that easy divorces were not pleasing to Allah. That said, the Qur'an does not require a man to show just cause to divorce his wife. It is relatively easy to do, although it does require a mandatory period of waiting to ensure against pregnancy:

> If you divorce your wives, divorce them at the end of their waiting period. Compute their waiting period and have fear of God, your Lord. You shall not expel them from your homes, nor shall they go away, unless they have committed a proven lewd act . . . if you have doubt concerning those of your wives who have ceased menstruating, know that their waiting period shall be three months . . . as for pregnant women, their term shall end with their confinement. God will ease the hardship of the man who fears him. (Sura 65:1-4)

Women also have the right to seek divorce in Islam, although the degree of difficulty is greater for the woman than for the man. A woman does not enjoy the ease of repeating "I divorce you" three times in front of witnesses and walking away from a marriage. A woman is required to follow a legal path in order to divorce, but may successfully terminate the marriage if her husband abuses or abandons her, is impotent, refuses to have sexual relations with her, or ceases supporting her financially. While the rules for divorce are patently unequal between men and women in Islam, it is also true that Islam treats women in higher regard than many cultures in the world, and Islam did greatly extend the overall rights of Arabian woman. Thomas Lippman writes,

> Divorced women may retain their personal property and anything their husbands have given them. Whatever property the husband agreed in the marriage contract to convey must be fully conveyed if there is a divorce, even if it was not fully conveyed at the time of the marriage. This is one of many examples of the way in which Shari'a ensures women's rights over their property. A woman's money, land, and property are her own, regardless of her marital status. (98)

POLYGAMY

The practice of polygamy, having multiple spouses, or more precisely polygyny, men having multiple wives, is an active facet of Islam. In societies where polygamy is legal, which would include all countries under *Shari'a* law, polygyny continues to be practiced. The Islamic custom of multiple wives came about primarily due to the high numbers of men lost in battle, which threatened the future of the movement. Polygyny was considered a benevolent act of kindness as many women were left without a companion or protector and faced uncertain futures. An element of honor also came to exist in this practice, as men were expected to fully marry a person they fell in love with rather than to take her on as a mistress. Simply taking a mistress would dishonor the first wife in the eyes of her family and of the greater community.

Muslim law dictates that men may have up to four wives if they are all treated equally. Maqsood lists the following prerequisites for having multiple wives:

- The first wife must give permission;
- Later wives must not be a cause of distress to earlier ones;
- Equal physical intimacy (or loving passion) is not something that is required (or possible), but the giving of equal time is;
- All wives must be treated fairly and equally as regards homes, food, clothing, gifts, and so on. Nights have to be spent with each in turn, unless a wife foregoes her turn. (215)

The Qur'an does seem to respect monogamy while at the same time allowing for multiple wives. Women are not allowed to have more than one husband at any point: "Marry such women as may seem good to you, two, three or four. But if you fear that you will not be able to act justly, then marry one woman" (Sura 4:3). Muhammad was monogamous and faithful to his first wife Khadijah for the twenty-five years they were together. After she died he married a variety of women for a variety of reasons, including love, tribal leverage, and political advantage. Muhammad received a special dispensation from Allah that allowed for unlimited wives, and over the rest of his life he married eleven other women.

The age of the female at marriage is also something that is culturally different and difficult for the twenty-first-century observer to comprehend. Muhammad gave his daughter Fatima to be married to Ali at the age of twelve. Muhammad's noted favorite wife after Khadijah was Aisha, who was six years old at marriage and nine when the marriage was consummated. These early marriages were a common element in pre-Islamic Arabia and were grafted into Muslim practices.

Apologists defend the Muslim practice of multiple wives as being consistent with leading Old Testament figures such as David and Solomon who also practiced polygamy. Robert Spencer takes the opposite approach by stating that Islamic polygamy encourages seeing women as commodities and that the Jewish and Christian standards have changed profoundly from the days of Solomon. Despite the polygamous past of Judaism, neither Jews nor Christians practice polygamy today (Spencer, 84). Amir Hussain posits that today approximately 95 percent of Muslims worldwide practice monogamy, and that the modern focus is on equity and fairness within the confines of one relationship (150–53).

TEMPORARY MARRIAGES

The very early Islamic practice of *muta*, a temporary marriage of convenience, was prevalent for several hundred years. The Shi'a term this as a "marriage of enjoyment," as it required a set time frame that could be as short as one hour. As is the case with polygamy, only men are allowed to initiate the *muta*. This allowance is not mentioned in the Qur'an but is covered in many of the Hadith. Sunni jurists disallowed the practice, citing instructions from Muhammad. Shi'a law schools also ended the practice until the Ayatollah Khomeini of Iran reaffirmed it in the twentieth century: "A woman may legally belong to a man in one of two ways, by continuing marriage or temporary marriage. In the former, the duration of the marriage need not be specified; in the latter, it must be stipulated, for example, that it is for a period of an hour, a day, a month, a year, or more" (Khomeini, 94). The ancient practice of *muta* is widely held by today's Muslims to be dishonorable and little more than sanctioned prostitution.

INTERFAITH MARRIAGE

In general, marriage between a Muslim and a *kirfir*, a non-Muslim, is discouraged. It is allowed in the case of Muslim men marrying a non-Muslim, especially if the person is a "Person of the Book." It is never proper for a Muslim woman to marry a non-Muslim man. The thought is that a non-Muslim man would not understand his wife's faith and that any children might not be brought up in the Islamic traditions. In the case of a mixed marriage between a Muslim man and a non-Muslim woman, the children must be raised Muslim. It is prohibited for a Muslim man or woman to marry a polytheist under any circumstances. Kenneth Craig reports that classic Islam "has achieved a remarkable degree of interracial coexistence" (254), which is associated to the belief that Abraham and Hagar were fully married as an interracial couple. Christians and Jews teach that Hagar was

Abraham's concubine rather than his wife, and that their relationship did not constitute marriage. Nevertheless, over the first few centuries Muslims enjoyed positive relationships with most other ethnic and faith groups.

THE BEATING OF WIVES

The Qur'an and other texts of Islam consistently teach that it is proper for men to administer corporal punishment to their wives:

> Men have authority over women because God has made the one superior to the other, and because they spend their wealth to maintain them. Good women are obedient. They guard their unseen parts because God has guarded them. As for those from whom you fear disobedience, admonish them, forsake them in beds apart, and beat them. Then if they obey you, take no further action against them. Surely God is high, supreme. (Sura 4:34)

John Bowker sees this verse as being merciful and not legalizing abuse, and one that needs to be taken literally. In order to reduce the occurrence of divorce and to keep the family unit intact, a husband is encouraged to first scold his wayward wife, next to send her into a secluded portion of the home, and finally, if neither works, he may beat her (Bowker, 127–28). To place this in historical perspective, pre-Islamic Arabia held women in such low esteem that wholesale abuse was prevalent. Islam reigned in the harsh culture of abuse by setting limits and guidelines. Additionally, there are arguments in Islam as to whether the verse should be taken as being purely symbolic. Hassaballa and Helminski write,

> Traditional authorities are virtually unanimous in asserting that this "striking" should be symbolic in nature and should be done only as an absolute last resort if the wife, according to the Prophet, "has become guilty, in an obvious manner, of immoral conduct." Also, the Prophet stressed that it should not cause pain; again, it should be a symbolic "nudge." (162)

Caner and Caner counter by citing Hadith 7: "Once the Prophet was asked about this subject, 'What rights does the woman have with the man?' He replied, 'He should feed her if he eats, clothe her when he dresses, avoid disfiguring her or beating her excessively or abandoning her except at home'" (138–39). The option to use corporal punishment on one's wife is a reality in Islam; it is also a reality that this option has been widely and systematically abused over the centuries. This is especially true of the modern fundamentalist regimes that have reverted to "pre-Islamic" practices toward women.

SEXUAL SIN

The Qur'an condemns all types of sexual sin, including fornication, adultery, and homosexuality. Islam expects monogamy within marriage to be the standard for society (it must be noted that multiple wives would be within that norm). Maqsood writes, "The practice of marriage is seen as the 'fortress' that protects people from being lured into immoral ways by their passionate urges" (168). The penalties for sexual sin are severe and are often carried out in the public arena. The sentence for adultery and fornication is one hundred lashes for both the man and woman, and the Hadith calls for stoning (3:535). Traditionally, homosexual activity also carries the death penalty. The Qur'an has much to say about homosexual practice: "Of all the creatures in the world, will you approach males and abandon those whom God created for you as mates" (26:165); "You satisfy your lust with men instead of women. Indeed you are a nation that has transgressed beyond bounds" (7:81). Christine Huda Dodge puts into perspective the harsh punishments for sexual sins, specifically homosexual practice: "In Islam, the harshest legal punishments are reserved for crimes that affect society as a whole. Muslims believe that homosexuality is a threat to the basic family structure, and therefore, a threat to society and a crime that must be punished as other crimes that affect society" (103).

In regressive Muslim societies, guilt or innocence has little to do with the penalties placed upon the female. The barbaric act of "honor" killings remains common in the most fundamentalist cultures. If a woman is raped, which occurs at alarming rates in many of these cultures, she is killed by family to remove the shame placed upon their name. Robert Spencer writes of the honor killing of a sixteen-year-old Jordanian girl who was raped by her brother. Her uncles decided that she had become too much of a disgrace to the family, so another brother slit her throat (*Islam Unveiled*, 91). Andrew Bushnell writes about the same issues in Pakistan:

> "Honor killing" is, in fact, well rooted in the Islamic world. It is by no means unheard of for a woman to be killed by her own family in order to "prosecute adultery." The absence of clarity about rape puts victims at risk of being doubly victimized, while their killers go unpunished. It was reported that in 2002, "the male head of a prominent Pakistani family murdered his daughter in a lawyer's office, only to be acquitted." (2)

All of Islam should not be painted with this brush, however, as moderate Muslims would see such actions as an affront to women and to the Qur'anic teachings. Spencer adds that in Saudi Arabia, one of the most conservative societies in the world, two men were arrested for the kidnapping and rape of a woman at gunpoint. The men were convicted and summarily beheaded (Spencer, *Islam Unveiled*, 92). This occurred in 2002 and could signal a shift in the status of women overall, especially in fundamentalist areas.

THE FUTURE OF WOMEN IN ISLAM

Overall, Muslims feel confident that the plight of women is improving, despite the regressive policies of the hyper-fundamentalist regimes. This issue, more than any other in Islam, will define the future of the religion in the West. The status of women will also factor into the future of the classic Muslim states: "In Saudi Arabia women are sexually segregated, required to be fully covered and are not allowed to drive cars. At the same time, there are more women than men in universities; Saudi women own their own companies and are major landowners" (Esposito, 99). In Egypt women may dress as they wish and are well represented in all professional areas. In *Teach Yourself Islam*, English convert to Islam Ruqaiyyah Waris Maqsood asks,

> How can anyone justify Islam's treatment of women, when it imprisons Afghans under blue shuttlecock burqas and makes Pakistani girls marry strangers against their will? How can you respect a religion that forces women into polygamous marriages, mutilates their genitals, forbids them to drive cars and subjects them to the humiliation of "instant" divorce? In fact, none of these practices are Islamic at all. (1)

Barazangi adds, "The traditional and prevailing Muslim emphasis of educating women in order for her [*sic*] to play merely a complimentary and domestic role contradicts the Qur'anic principles and is in discord with the realities of Muslim women" (1).

Twenty-first-century Islam continues to be mired in the age-old problem of breaking away from its once progressive structure for women. All great movements are sooner or later forced to contextualize, to reassess, and to change appropriately in order to remain relevant. This has occurred in pre-revolution Iran, in Egypt, and in Turkey. However, with the Wahabbi-inspired Taliban and certain African regimes, the world has seen a veritable reclaiming of "the golden day of the Prophet" and a return to "true Islam." This seems to be the single greatest disconnect in modern Islam. Is a return to the fundamental environs of the days of Muhammad actually possible after the passage of fourteen hundred years? And is this regressive focus a liability to twenty-first-century women?

> A woman came to Allah's Apostle and said, 'O Allah's Apostle! Men only benefit from your teachings, so please devote to us from some of your time, a day on which we may come to you so that you may teach us of what Allah has taught you.' Allah's Apostle said, 'Gather on such-and-such a day at such-and-such a place.' They gathered and Allah's Apostle came to them and taught them of what Allah had taught him. (Bukhari)

CHAPTER EIGHT

Religion of Peace?

Is Islam a religion of peace or an inherently violent religion? This two-part question has been asked countless times since Tuesday, September 11, 2001. The attacks on that day in New York and Washington, DC, and the crash of Flight 93 outside Shanksville, Pennsylvania, placed Islam in a defensive position of unparalleled scope. Were those nineteen men acting as true Muslims who were following the teachings of the Qur'an, or were they crazed zealots who used God as a convenient justification for their acts of terrorism? Is it possible to be a true Muslim and a cold-blooded terrorist simultaneously? A further question makes this quandary even more difficult to understand: Why do Muslims kill each other in the name of Allah and jihad?

As is the case with many questions related to Islam, the answer to most of these questions lies somewhere between the polarizations. Islam can be viewed as both a peaceful religion and one that has a history of great violence. This would certainly be the case if one attempted to answer these questions using only the Qur'an as a source. The Qur'an and Hadith each contain verses that command peace toward all people. Conversely, the texts also sanction extreme violence against any person or group that threatens the *umma*. Which is the genuine Islam? That specific question is the hardest facet of Islam to understand for the Western observer. This issue is made even more difficult when contrasting Islam with Christianity, the primary faith of those in the West.

The Qur'an does indeed make contradictory statements on war and peace in the pursuit of serving Allah. In the early era of Muhammad's ministry, he preached a message of monotheism and an equality of all people, including Christians and Jews. Over time his unique message was disregarded by the masses, forcing Muhammad and his small band of followers to flee Mecca for Medina. At that point, the message of Muhammad took on more of a militaristic tone. It was also in the Medinan period that Islam began raiding caravans from Syria and doing battle with forces that threatened the movement. The majority of battles were fought between Muhammad's followers and his ancestral tribe in Mecca. These battles framed the later years of Muhammad's life, resulting in the conquest of Mecca and, ultimately, control of the entire Arabian Peninsula. This period can be summarized by the revelation found in the Qur'an as Sura 22:39-40:

> Permission is given to fight those upon whom war is made, who were wronged. Truly God is well able to help them, those who were driven out of their homes unjustly, simply because they said our Lord is God. Did not God use some people to repel others, or else monasteries and churches and synagogues and mosques where the name of God is constantly mentioned would have been pulled down? Truly God will help those who help God. Surely God is almighty.

JIHAD

The concept and theology of jihad also changed during the latter portion of Muhamad's life. The Arabic word *jihad* derives from the verb *jahada*, which means "he strove." A literal rendering of the word would be "to strive or exert against an enemy." Originally, the enemy in question was inside each individual. A good Muslim was to do battle with the desires and motivations that naturally led away from Allah's will for life. Each Muslim is taught to exert and strive daily against the internal struggle, or as Frog and Amy Orr-Ewing put it, "to wage war against the carnal soul" (31).

In the Medinan years Muhammad received revelations that he understood as justifying militaristic action against the Meccans, non-Arabs, and later the Jews. This justification was also tied into the

concept of jihad. To Muhammad, the larger jihad was the inner struggle against carnal humanity. At this level, Islam is an intensely personal
religion. The lesser jihad was the defense of the faith that justified violence, war, and the taking of life. Over time, this concept grew to
include progressive conquests of other lands. The lesser jihad is
extremely difficult to explain away as anything other than holy war,
although the attempt has been made by many apologists post 9/11:
"The outer (lesser) jihad is the effort to make one's society reflect the
principles of submission to God" (Hussain, 117). The quandary lies in
how one accomplishes this task.

The practice of abrogation also confuses this matter for the
Western observer. While neither the Old Testament nor New
Testament utilizes abrogation, the Qur'an is built upon it. If a revelation was provided to Muhammad contradicting an earlier one, the
later revelation would effectively cancel the earlier ones. Riddell and
Cotterell explain abrogation this way: "The theory of abrogation, canceling out one passage by a later passage where the two appear to be
contradictory, seeks to resolve apparent conflicts and contradictions. A
passage from the Medina period would abrogate an earlier Meccan
one" (61).

The Qur'an was written in neither chronological nor logical order.
The 114 suras are arranged by length, from longest to shortest (with
the exception of the first sura, which is viewed as an opening prayer).
To make this structure even more confusing, the longest suras tend to
be later chronologically, but are placed in the front of the Qur'an.
Which verses remain operative to Islam, those that promote peace or
those that counsel violence?

It seems that many Muslims choose to read the Qur'an as they see
fit, seemingly ignoring the issues brought about by abrogation. Even a
skillful reader of the Qur'an would find it difficult to be precise when
navigating through the non-chronological text. As a result, the Qur'an
is read as an instrument of peace by those who wish for it to be that,
and a declaration of violence for those who seek such justification. The
Qur'an simply allows for both options. When citing abrogated verses,
the majority opinion seems to be that the "Sword Verse," Sura 9:5,
allows for slaying idolaters by ambush and, due to its later date, abro-

gates 124 earlier verses. If this is true, Sura 9:5 cancels the more peaceful commands for unity among all of God's peoples. Again, is this a
legitimate entrée to war and conflict by Muslims, especially when
innocent life is sacrificed in the process?

At this point we see the majority opinion shift away from the most
literal reading of the Qur'an and find that the "whole" of the text is
taken into account. The majority opinion will continue to support
conflict, but any and all conflict must meet certain criteria to be
justified holy war. John Esposito, executive director of the Center
for Muslim-Christian Understanding, cites the guidelines for justifiable war:

> As the Muslim community grew, questions quickly emerged as to
> what was proper behavior during times of war. The Qur'an provided
> guidelines and regulations regarding the conduct of war: who is to
> fight and who is exempted (48:17), (9:91), when hostilities must
> cease (2:192), and how prisoners should be treated (47:4). Most
> important, verses such as 2:294 emphasized that warfare and the
> response to violence and aggression must be proportional:
> "Whoever transgresses against you, respond in kind." (120)

Thomas Lippman writes, "Islam teaches believers to take action
when they feel the faith is threatened" (179). He sums up a portion of
the majority opinion, but leaves out the most puzzling aspect of justified conflict. Traditionally, jihad in the militaristic sense was proper for
either defense or for expansion. The defense of Islam is a logical justification for a war. This would be uniquely accurate after considering
that classic Islam does not separate mosque and state. Muslims, over
the early centuries, did use war for the sake of extending the reach of
Islam. Frog and Amy Orr-Ewing sum up the Muslim understanding
of violence in this manner:

> The meaning here (Sura 48:16) is that Muslims should fight until
> their oppressors embrace Islam. In the early days of Islam, the faith
> was indeed spread by the sword. Those who did not embrace Islam
> were killed. Such instances are recorded in the Hadith: "Allah's
> Apostle said, 'The hour will not be established until you fight with

the Jews, and the stone behind you which a Jew will be hiding will say, O Muslim! There is a Jew hiding behind me, so kill him.'" Jihad is thus an instrument of Islamic mission and, if necessary, can be used for the defense of Islam. It is an armed struggle used as an instrument to establish or defend Islamic social order. (32)

Islam's regulations for holy war grew over the final years of Muhammad's leadership. The expansion of the movement was to adhere to certain and specific regulations that did not allow for indiscriminate killing. Despite this expectation, unbelievers were sometimes killed upon refusal to convert. The Hadith records an example of a Jewish man who was killed due to refusing Muhammad's message: "The Prophet was reciting from the Qur'an at Mecca and prostrated while reciting it, and those who were with him did the same except an old man who took a handful of small stones or earth and lifted it to his forehead and said, 'This is sufficient for me.' Later on, I saw him killed as a non-believer" (2:100).

The Medinan period saw Muslims and Jews become bitter enemies. At one point Muhammad was open to the Jews and meshed Muslim practices with those of the Hebrews. As the Medinan Jews began to reject the prophethood of Muhammad, he broke with them in every possible way. Jews who refused to convert were exiled and one tribe was executed for treason. After Muhammad's death Islam conquered Palestine, and the animosity has played out in various wars and struggles from that point forward.

A person who renounces Islam is deemed an apostate and is to be summarily killed. Phil Parshall writes, "The law of apostasy is thus spelled out with unmistakable clarity. Conversion to Islam is not only encouraged but at times has been forcibly induced. Conversion from Islam is punishable by instant death" (107). In early Islam this seems to have been the injunction that was most consistently applied. It is also taught that Muslims are never to battle with fellow Muslims. In Muhammad's time this would have been an unthinkable occurrence, but shortly after his death this reality became both real and deadly. A civil war accompanied the official schism between Sunni and Shi'a Islam. Islam has not recovered from the mutual hatred brought about by the succession issues. Historically, neither group has viewed the other as being truly Muslim, which has allowed for "justified" conflict within the teachings of Islam.

A further thought pertains to the notion of God's divine favor being displayed through successful conquest. Early Islam saw its rapid expansion as being divinely orchestrated. Charles Kimball explains,

> The expansion of Islam was understood as the establishment of God's rule. And the rapid spread of Islam—going west across North Africa and into Spain; north through the Fertile Crescent; and east through the Tigris and Euphrates Valley, across Persia and into Northern India—within the first hundred years following Muhammad's death was an unprecedented and stunning develop-ment in world history. (177)

The belief that "successful expansion equals God's favor" led Muslims to see the world in two diametrically different spheres: the House of Islam and the House of War. All areas not yet under the dominion of Allah and Islam were deemed the "House of War," and were thus "nec-essary" conquests. If God was ordaining and empowering Islam to expand with both might and speed, it must have been God's will for Islam eventually to cover the globe. After all, Muhammad saw himself preaching the restoration of Christianity and the natural extension of Judaism. Islam was God's plan for the world through the Muslims.

Rollin Armour, Sr., expounds on this theme:

> The first [House of War] is the Islamic area proper, where ideally speaking, all have surrendered or submitted to God as Muslims or, if not, have at least submitted to Islamic rule and thus to God's law in society. While Muslims did not require the people they conquered to convert to Islam, they presumed their subjects would eventually do so, and they believed, furthermore, that Islam would eventually cover the entire world. (31–32)

Compared to Christianity, Islam does have a pronounced mili-taristic tone, but Christians should not fail to remember the Crusades. During the Crusades, all sorts of unsavory acts took place and each was done in the name of God. Does this make Christianity an inherently violent religion? Judaism also doesn't fare well when held to the criterion of violence. Jews and Christians alike tend to see the violence of the Old Testament as playing against God's overarching plan for the Jews. The Jews, however, are pressed to defend the work of the Zealots. This fundamentalist group killed Christians and Roman citizens in the name of their faith. Islam is a religion with a history of violence and forced expansion. Islam is also a religion that has consistently taught peace and reconciliation for all people. The early Jews and Christians were allowed to accept a secondary status and pay a tax to Muslim leaders in exchange for the right to worship and practice their faith.

All religions, including Christianity and Judaism, have histories of violence and regrettable acts done in the name of God. Islam is no exception and is arguably the most violent of the three in the historical sense. Islam is also, however, a religion that upheld peace with a purpose that is larger than humanity. So it is possible for one Muslim to cite Islam as a religion of peace while another advances the call of jihad for the faith. Simply put, Islam can be both peaceful and warlike simultaneously. For the Muslim, those seemingly incongruent positions can be reconciled, but only if the conflict meets certain criteria and guidelines. Herein lies the issue for contemporary Islam: are terrorists genuine Muslims practicing genuine Islam? The peaceful aspects of Islam have been virtually erased over the past twenty years by the work of terrorists acting in the name of Allah. Does this accurately define Islam?

CHAPTER NINE

Radical Islam

TERRORISTS

It would be safe to say that many Westerners see Islam as a violent religion populated by terrorists. The reality might be somewhat different, but perception defines reality, especially in this new century where wars are fought live on cable television. Muslims, Jews, and Christians are each victims of the stereotyping that pervades our snap-judgment world.

It is obvious that early Islam expanded by the sword and that conflict was the norm. This would also be historically accurate of virtually all expansionist movements of that era. The pressing question would concern what this fourteen-hundred-year-old religion looks like today. Thirty years ago the answer to that question would have been quite different than it is now. Islam, and Muslims in general, was not a focus of the world's attention thirty years ago. The focus shifted when a fundamentalist and regressive brand of Islam roared onto the scene. Today, Islam is broadly painted in the West by such terror-driven Muslims.

Renowned Middle East scholar Bernard Lewis writes, "Most Muslims are not fundamentalists, and most fundamentalists are not terrorists, but most present-day terrorists are Muslims and proudly identify themselves as such" (137). Christianity is also a source of acts of violence and terror, from the Crusades to the Irish war between Protestants and Catholics to the abortion clinic bombers; but these are often characterized differently than modern Muslim radicals. These

Christian outbreaks do not seek a return to the first century of the church or to the "exactness" of the faith in its formative years. Radical Islam seeks just that, a regressive return to the ideals of the era of Muhammad. Plus, many Christian "terrorists" have not avowed their fight to be holy. Muslim terrorists blatantly cite jihad and holy war as being synonymous and often invoke them simultaneously. Bruce Lawrence adds:

> For the militant Muslim minority, the necessary sequel to professing faith is defending the faith. Instead of daily prayer, alms-giving, fasting and pilgrimage—all deemed to be essential practices, or pillars of piety, for most Muslims—the very next step required of all believers, in the view of militants, is to wage jihad. They justify jihad not as moral struggle but as all-out war. Citing certain passages from the Qur'an, they uphold them as singular in meaning and valid for all time. The duty of every believer is to sacrifice himself or herself in defense of the faith through armed combat. (16)

The Qur'an does indeed require jihad of all Muslims, and that requirement could, at some point, include the taking up of arms to defend the faith. The Qur'an does not, however, require a lifestyle of combat with an apocalyptic mindset. Jihad for defense or expansion would also be an end in and of itself, and not a means to the nebulous end sought by most modern Muslim fundamentalists. Early Islam saw its mandate as placing the known world under the dominion of Allah. While the Western observer might have trouble with both the theology and practice of this facet of jihad, many of today's Muslims see the terrorist version as an absolute aberration of the Qur'anic teachings. Bruce Lawrence typifies Muslim terrorists as "absolutists who speak only for the fractious minority who stress the confrontational aspects of monotheistic faith" (16). He goes on to contrast a moderate Muslim as "those open to engagement with non-Muslims for the purpose of seeking allies in a larger war against poverty, racism and environmental degradation" and "as one who seeks a world of peace where the true jihad is for justice, not armed conflict motivated by hatred or displayed as terror" (17).

Time produced a 2004 special edition focusing on the modern struggle within Islam. An early sentence reads, "The vast majority of the world's more than one billion practicing Muslims are peaceful citizens getting on with their lives" (54). This view is widely held, but it leads to the difficult question of how many radical Muslims exist in the world. It would be impossible to be definitive on this, but it would certainly seem to be a minority of the world's 1.2 billion Muslims. This minority, however, is vocal, active, and in control of the world's attention. This group also defines Islam for much of the non-Muslim world.

Montgomery Watt demonstrates five assertions of contemporary Muslim fundamentalists:

> A static world, which requires no concept of development.
> The finality of Islam: no further revelation is needed, no other system possible.
> Islam is self-sufficient. It owes nothing, needs nothing, from any other political, economic, social or religious system. Education is simply the passing on of received knowledge.
> Islam will produce a universal *dar al-Islam* (House of Islam) backed by *Shari'a* law.
> Muhammad himself and the history of early Islam is sanitized and idealized to provide the pattern for the only viable and valid pattern for life today. (*Muhammad at Medina*, 1)

A hotly debated issue since September 11, 2001, has been whether today's Muslim terrorists are truly Islamic. The answer will always be elusive to non-Muslim Westerners, so the best approach would be to question the motivation for terrorism. It would also assist the understanding of terrorism to ask if suicide is permitted in Islam. Brad Hoffman defines a terrorist as "Someone for which violence is first and foremost a sacramental act or divine duty executed in direct response to some theological demand or imperative" (65). Demy and Stewart add, "In their thinking, not only is their mission performed in the name of God, but it actually originates in the mind of God and the will of God, and is then passed on to the terrorists as God's special agents on earth. The terrorists believe they are acting in the name of

God" (67). Today's Muslim terrorists believe they are acting in the name of Allah and in the best interests of both Islam and the world. Many also seem to be more than willing to sacrifice their lives in the process, and, sadly, the lives of other people as well. Jeurgensmeyer sums it up this way:

> They [terrorists] are all about destruction, of course, but more importantly they are about human destruction on behalf of a divine act. For that reason, they are related; each can be explained in terms of the others. Sacrifice can be regarded as a symbolic form of noble self-destruction [martyrdom]; martyrdom can be seen as the internalization of sacrifice or of war; and religious warfare can be viewed as a litany of sacrifice and martyrdom. (104)

MARTYRS

Believers willing to sacrifice their lives for their cause are not unique to Islam or to religion in general. Muslim martyrs do, however, define the past forty years of world terrorism. Jihad as holy war has come to include the concept of *shahid*, which is martyrdom for the cause of Allah. Literally meaning "the one who testified," the *shahid* gives up his or her life for Allah, and, as a result, is given automatic entry into Paradise. Muhammad received this revelation while on the battlefield, and from that point forward, the act of holy war changed forever. With the prize of Paradise awaiting each martyr, the ultimate sacrifice in pursuit of the cause became a sweeter pursuit. Frog and Amy Orr-Ewing outline Muslim martyrdom this way:

> The shahid is one who has testified to his faith upon the battlefield, and he is promised that he will in turn witness God (4:70). The Qur'an assures Muslims that martyrs will be shown favor. If someone has been slain in the way of God he will experience joy, bounty and blessing (3:164), and can expect to pass into paradise with certainty, avoiding the punishment of the grave. In a religion that is generally ambiguous about who will be saved, this theological certainty is incredibly attractive. For the zealous Muslim who is yearning for heaven and not hell, there is no certainty that good

deeds will outweigh bad on the day of judgment. Only martyrdom in a jihad can promise this elusive assurance. (33)

Both the Qur'an and Hadith deal with the subject of martyrdom and, as such, it has been part of Islam since the early era. Despite the subsequent fourteen hundred years of martyrs for the faith, the twentieth century saw the act elevated to a significant instrument of warfare. Hasan al-Banna (1906–1949), founder of the Muslim Brotherhood of Egypt and ideological forerunner of al-Qaeda, is memorialized on a website with these words:

Allah is our objective.
The messenger is our leader.
Qur'an is our law.
Jihad is our way.
Dying in the way of Allah is our highest hope. (Cox and Marks, 52)

Who are these martyrs who are so willing to die for Islam? Soon after 9/11 it was thought that the *shahid* was from the uneducated and underprivileged classes. Over the past few years that assertion has been challenged as many educated professionals have sacrificed their lives in terrorist acts. J. F. Legrain comments, "It may be surprising to some that these emergent groups within Islam are not economically or intellectually disadvantaged" ("Hamas," 414). Daniel Pipes adds, "I also wish to note that Islamism has few connections to wealth and poverty; it is not a response to deprivation. There is no discernable connection between income and Islamism" (18).

Whether the martyr is poor and uneducated or privileged and professional, the result is often the same. The person dies for the cause and, in so doing, kills as many people as possible in the process. Today, successful martyrs are those who take the maximum number of additional lives, especially among infidels (non-Muslims). This is unarguably the point at which modern jihad veers away from the Qur'an. The holy text of Islam lays down strict guidelines for holy war. It is always unlawful for the Muslim to kill noncombatants. Reza Alsan writes, "The killing of women, children, monks, rabbis, the elderly, or any other noncombatants was absolutely forbidden under any circumstances" (84). Obviously, the modern Muslim radical who kills by stealth and indiscriminate means breaks with Qur'anic teachings. This would especially be true of the stipulation against suicide.

Suicide is a significant sin for the Muslim. Huraira's version of the Hadith states, "Whoever purposely throws himself from a mountain and kills himself will be in the [Hell] Fire, falling down into it and abiding therein perpetually forever; and whoever drinks poison and kills himself with it, he will be carrying his poison in his hand and drinking it in the [Hell] Fire wherein he will abide in forever" (7:450). Islam sees Allah alone as the giver and taker of life; therefore, whoever commits suicide will not be eligible for salvation: "Historically, both Sunni and Shiite Muslims have generally forbidden 'sacrificial religious suicide' and acts of terrorism. However, in the late twentieth century, both groups came to equate suicide bombing with martyrdom" (Esposito, 125). This shift in understanding has elevated sacrificial suicide to absolute martyr status and encourages willing *shahid* to die for Islam in order to access Paradise. Willing *shahid*, therefore, are not seen as committing suicide, but martyrdom, and told they will achieve Paradise rather than eternal damnation.

WHY IS ISLAM VIOLENT?

There are many theories as to why modern radical Muslims are increasingly violent and why so many are willing to die for Islam. Mawdudi was an early twentieth-century Islamist who advocated for *Shari'a* states across the globe. He wrote, "The goal of Islam is to rule the entire world and submit all of mankind to the faith of Islam. Any nation and power in this world that tries to get in the way of that goal, Islam will fight and destroy" (Lewis, 72). This doctrine would align with the House of War concept and Allah's will for Islam to permeate the world. This long-held belief pales in contrast to many contemporary issues that seem to drive radical Muslim terrorists. Osama bin Laden personifies today's radical Muslim terrorist. He demonstrates a virulent hatred for the West and for Israel. He also cites America's occupations in Saudi Arabia, Kuwait, and Iraq as acts of aggression and thus a declaration of war against Allah and Islam. His *fatwa* against America calls all Muslims to kill the Americans and their allies, civilians and military, in order to liberate the places where holy mosques exist and in order to remove them from all Muslim lands:

> We—with God's help—call on every Muslim who believes in God and wishes to be rewarded to comply with God's order to kill the Americans and plunder their money whenever and wherever they find it. We call on Muslim ulema, leaders, youth, and soldiers to launch the raid on Satan's US troops and the devil's supporters allying with them, and to displace those who are behind them so that they may learn a lesson. (Ibrahim, 13)

Al-Qaeda and other modern radical groups coalesce around the goals of establishing a Palestinian state and destroying Israel. Demy and Stewart write, "Among the long-term goals of al-Qaeda are promoting a worldwide jihad that destroys non-Islamic states and establishes societies, cultures, and states around the globe that will be governed by Islamic law. One of the most striking innovations of bin Laden's brand of international terrorism has been a vision of a holy war, or jihad, that excludes any possibility of compromise" (109).

The anti-colonialism, anti-imperialism, and anti-Western motives of radical Islam have inspired several terrorist organizations. The Palestinian Liberation Organization, or PLO, was formed in the 1970s as a secular group fighting for an independent Palestinian state. This is the only major Islamic organization that considers itself secular rather than religious. Hezbollah, or the Islamic Jihad, is a mixture of Arab and Lebanese Muslims with strong ties to Iranian Shiites. Hezbollah exists to remove the Israeli state from Palestine and to create a fully Muslim society in Lebanon. The 1982 invasion of Israel into Lebanon was the primary catalyst for the full radicalization of Hezbollah. As is typical of Shiite Muslims, Hezbollah enforces the pathos of oppression and injustice against Islam by Israel and the West. Hamas is a Sunni organization founded in 1987 in order to remove Israel from Palestine.

Each group cites America's unqualified support for Israel as a prime source of their anti-Western motivations. They also see America as demonstrating a double standard in sanctioning Pakistan for developing nuclear capability but ignoring the same achievement by both Israel and India. Many Muslims also see the moral laxity of America and the West as testament to the need for a world based on Shari'a. Aside from a virulent hatred of Israel as "occupiers" of Palestine, fundamentalist Muslims also see their jihad as defending Islam against the morally corrupted West. Osama bin Laden has carefully fostered the ongoing rhetoric of Islam being under attack by the West as reason to take up arms in every region of the world. This is reminiscent of the days of Muhammad's faithful fighting of the Meccans, which seems to be the reason he stresses this agenda. This approach harkens back to a pure time in Islam when the *umma* were undivided, when the message was clear, and when the enemy was clearly defined:

> With each of these further terrorist strikes, pretexts given by the groups claiming responsibility included the need to respond to western military incursions into Muslim lands. Other statements by al-Qaeda, however, suggested that radical motivations were connected with a much bigger agenda. A statement by Osama bin Laden shows that he and his supporters saw the conflict as being between the West and Islam: "Under no circumstances should we forget this enmity between us and the infidels. For, the enmity is based on creed. God says: Never will the Jews or the Christians be satisfied with thee unless thou follow their form of religion. It is a question of faith, not a war against terrorism, as Bush and Blair try to depict it." (Riddell, *Christians and Muslims*, 47)

Today's enemy is difficult to identify but incredibly easy to vilify. This would be true for Muslims and non-Muslims alike. Osama bin Laden has actually made the rationale for his escalating war too simplistic: "Classic Islamic theology divided the world, as bin Laden has, into two realms—the House of Islam and the House of War. He made this clear in his statements on November 1, 2001: 'The world has been divided into two camps: one under the banner of the cross, as Bush, the head of infidelity said, and another under the banner of Islam'" (Catherwood, 177). In reality, Christianity has not declared war on Islam, nor does any American president "lead" the religion.

Simple seems to work for bin Laden, however, as the Hydra now has many fewer heads.

Radical Islam's terrorism is a genuine departure from the Qur'an and the norm of early Islam. Islam has always been prone to violence, but it also operated under stated guidelines. Each and every guideline has been broken by these modern radicals in pursuit of defending their faith and religion from incursion and corruption. Osama bin Laden's al-Qaeda is as far removed from orthodox Islam as Jim Jones's cult was from Christianity. Many leading Muslim clerics and scholars have condemned al-Qaeda, Hezbollah, the PLO, and Hamas as operating outside the mainstream of orthodox Islam. While this is a potentially deadly stance, it is an important element of reigning in radical Muslims from within Islam.

CHAPTER TEN

The Future

SO GOES ISLAM, SO GOES THE WORLD

It is a sobering exercise to consider the short- and long-term future of our world. Conflict based on religion or ideology is rampant, and most is related to Islam. Twenty-five percent of the world's population is Muslim, and the vast majority live outside the Middle East. As Thomas Lippman reports,

> The vast majority of Muslims are not Arabs and not wealthy. The three biggest Muslim nations are Indonesia, with about 172 million Muslims; Pakistan, with 118 million; and Bangladesh, with 100 million. The list of countries of which the population is more than half Muslim includes Mali, Afghanistan, Malaysia, Albania, and of course, Iran, none of them Arab. And many Arabs in Syria, Lebanon, and Palestine are Christians, not Muslims. (viii)

A. Christian Van Gorder adds, "Over one billion people in sixty countries call themselves Muslim" (11). It is clear that Islam is not an Arab-dominated religion any longer. Islam has shared the world with other people and religious groups for centuries. Today, however, this mandatory coexistence is growing increasingly tenuous due to radical and aggressive expressions of Islam.

Several questions surface when one considers the current status of the world order. Is it possible for Muslims, Christians, and Jews to live in some semblance of peace in the future? Is it possible for Shi'a and

Sunni Muslims truly to come together under the umbrella of the *umma*? Is it possible for the disparate Muslim countries to create opportunity for different people groups to practice their religions in the fashion of early Islam? Will the genocide being practiced in the Darfur region be both condemned and stopped from within Islam? Will Israel continue to be the flash point between Islam and the West? Does Christianity have any hope of achieving meaningful and productive dialogue with Islam? The answers to these questions will go far in determining the future of our world. Many of these issues are effectively beyond the capabilities of Islam, Judaism, and Christianity.

The gulf between the three great world religions is so large that some level of tolerance is the only viable option. This option of tolerance is far-reaching at best as the inherent differences are so great. There is no reason to sugarcoat these dire realities when genuinely assessing the state of religion in the world. To be elementary and overly simplistic, the world is a royal mess. Islam's history with the Jews is one of mutual hatred, which was exacerbated with the formation of the State of Israel in the 1940s. Both groups view the other as interloper and aggressor, making this the wedge issue for most of fundamentalist Islam. Islam sees the West as the prime corrupter of Islamic ideals and as blindly supporting Israel. Intra-Islam conflict is at historically high levels, especially in Iraq and in the African regions. Christians know little about Islam as a religion or Muslims as people. The same could be said about the majority of Muslims and their knowledge of Christianity. Blended and distilled, these realities leave few options for solving the religious and ideological crises facing the world of the twenty-first century.

If it is accurate that few options exist, then each possibility must be explored and advanced in an attempt to stem the tide of violence and chaos that plagues humankind. It is safe to say that theological differences will always separate the three religions, so the answer does not reside in theology. Geographical issues will also continue to exist as long as Israel and the Palestinians share land they each claim as solely their own. Drawing lines and boundaries will not solve the problems either, as one group ultimately will be disenfranchised. As long as each group is willing to fight for the its holy land, geographical decisions won't suffice. Solving the issues within Islam does not seem to be the answer, as the *umma* is more orthodox and historical than actual. Plus, only Muslims can solve intra-Islamic problems, and this would require a significant number of Muslims to commit to doing so. Riddell and Cotterell accentuate the difficulties facing Islam due to differences between moderate Muslims and the more fundamentalist clerics:

> Any reformation in Islamic thinking along the lines of that called for by many moderate Islamic thinkers would need to address not only the threat posed by radical Islamist activists, but also the stranglehold on authority held by the group of traditionalist conservative clergy who are entrenched in positions of religious power at various levels throughout the Muslim world. (209)

This reality in modern Islam not only highlights the distance between the retro-Islamism promoted by clerics and the post-modern attempts of moderate Muslims, but also the historic divide between the Sunni and Shiite Muslims. Neither Christianity nor Western ideals can factor into solving that issue. Christianity may, however, have a role in bringing a greater level of peace and hope to today's world. This potential hope lies in a greater understanding and tolerance of Islam in general, and individual Muslims in particular. This won't be achieved by Christianity as a monolithic movement, however, as Christianity is fragmented in more ways than Islam. The fundamentalist branch of Christianity will have a much more difficult time understanding Islam and dialoguing with Muslims than will moderate Christians. Fundamentalist Christian groups tend to be pro-Israel in order to hasten the return of Christ, which is a main tenet of dispensational premillennial theology. This seems to be a disingenuous reason to promote Israel and to demonize Islam, but this is the doctrine of much of the Christian Right. The hope for greater understanding, tolerance, and dialogue will occur only if it begins in the moderate middle of both Christianity and Islam.

One answer would be to expand on the work of the 1993 Parliament of the World's Religions. This group came together to discuss the myriad religious issues affecting the world and to provide guidelines for increased tolerance among religions. Swiss Roman Catholic theologian Hans Kung created a document that called for an ecumenical progress toward peace. His work was so overwhelmingly endorsed that it became the signature piece of this group. The Declaration of a Global Ethic was published that year and remains a roadmap for ecumenical peace for the creation of a true world peace.

> There will be no peace among the peoples of this world without peace among the world religions.
> There will be no peace among the world religions without peace among the Christian churches.
> The community of the Church is an integral part of the world community. Ecumenism ad intra, concentrated on the Christian world, and ecumenism ad extra, oriented toward the whole inhabited earth, are interdependent.
> Peace is indivisible: it begins within us. (quoted in Drummond, 194)

Kung went on to say, "We must treat others (regardless of religion) as we wish others to treat us" (195). This would seem to be a major step in the progression of toleration and dialogue. A level of mutual respect based on the belief in God will always be necessary for dialogue among the various and disparate religions, especially when the belief structures greatly differ. No ground will be made if one religion is intransigent and unilateral in its belief structure. This is an obvious problem for Muslim extremists such as Osama bin Laden who allow for no compromise of any form. That said, many Christians view the study of Islam as an affront to Jesus, even if the study will ultimately allow for both understanding and ministry. Kung concludes the document with these words: "Earth cannot be changed for the better unless the consciousness of individuals is changed first" (196). Again, this seems to be the key for future peace among world religions, especially Islam, Judaism, and Christianity. This question remains, however: which group will take the lead in saving the world from religion?

THERE IS NO PLACE LIKE HOME

It seems reasonable to believe that the most productive dialogue would take place in the West among Muslims and non-Muslims, especially Christians. Christianity is built upon a belief in the inclusiveness of God. Christian theology supports extending God's love to all people, especially those who have differing beliefs. These facts should also become a starting point for a joint understanding of the differences between Islam and Christianity. Rather than being a point of contention, and an exercise in which group is most wrong, a focus on commonalities could act in the opposite way. A. Christian Van Gorder suggests this approach:

> Framing the Muslim-Christian interaction with the question "Do we worship the same God?" is too simplistic. It is more helpful to ask, "What kind of God is revealed in Christianity and in Islam?" Though the traditions agree that God is One, they diverge widely on how that Oneness is expressed. This fact is vital to Muslims and an important starting point for dialogue. Christianity begins with "God is love," and Islam teaches that "God is One." Christianity calls individuals to enter a covenant relationship with God. Islam calls individuals to worshipfully assume a proper place of obedience before God's will and revelation. (15–16)

The shared central focus is God. It would be hard to create a better beginning point for discussion and dialogue than the reality of a transcendent God.

At the end of the day, Muslims and Christians will continue to disagree on the person of Jesus. To the Muslim, Jesus was a great prophet who was taken up to Paradise to await a return that will signal the looming end of time. To the Christian, Jesus is God Incarnate, the Son of God, and the Messiah-Savior. Muslims do not believe Jesus was crucified and, consequentially, believe he did not resurrect from the dead. Christians believe Jesus was crucified, buried, resurrected, and ascended to heaven, each for the purpose of bringing salvation to humankind. Muslims believe Muhammad was the final prophet and, as such, supersedes Jesus. These are not small theological differences, and neither Christians nor Muslims are likely to give up their belief system. Each group can, however, be more open to the beliefs of the other without compromising their unique theologies. It would pay dividends to consider the words of George W. Braswell on this point: "A Christian response to Muslim peoples is surrounded by the teachings of Jesus Christ and the apostle Paul because the Christian has been called to follow the Way, the Truth, and the Life" (132). The New Testament clearly teaches the necessity of the Christian to be propelled by love. A closer reading demonstrates the "fine print" of the Christian scriptures; to love all people with the same love God provides each Christian.

QUESTIONS AND ANSWERS

Do Muslims worship the same God as Christians and Jews?

While this is a point of contention in the West, it is clear that Muhammad believed Allah was indeed the Most High God of the Jews and Christians and that Islam was the extension of both expressions of faith. Muslims believe that Muhammad was God's final prophet, providing God's words to humankind for a final time.

What does "Islam" mean?

Islam means "submission," as in "surrender to God." There are Muslims who define Islam as meaning "peace." The root of both Islam and peace is the same in Arabic, *salam.* However, the proper definition is "submission."

How many Muslims live in the world today?

There are more than 1.2 billion Muslims; the vast majority live outside of the Middle East. Indonesia has the largest Muslim population with more than 200 million. Muslim populations are expanding over much of the world, including in the United States. Peter Riddell reports, "The UK Muslim population increased from approximately 400,000 to 1.6 million between 1975 and 2001, an increase of 300%. In contrast, the Christian population in the UK increased by only 9% during the same time span" (*Christians and Muslims*, 34).

Do Muslims believe in Jesus?

Islam teaches that Jesus was a great prophet who brought Allah's revelation to the Jews some six hundred years before Muhammad. The Qur'an mentions Jesus thirty-five times, including the Virgin Birth, miracles, and specific teachings. Muslims believe Jesus was miraculously taken to Paradise rather than being crucified, and will return to signal the coming apocalypse. Muslims do not believe that Jesus was the Son of God or was in any manner divine.

What is the importance of Islam being a monotheistic religion?

As a formal religion, Islam began with Allah's revelations to Muhammad in 610 CE. Muhammad taught a faith based solely on the One God, just as Abraham taught centuries earlier. Pre-Islamic Arabia was a pagan society where each tribe and clan worshiped multiple gods and goddesses. Muhammad's message was not received well by the pagan tribal leaders of Mecca. The *Kaa'bah*, the cube-like structure that housed the 360 idols worshiped in Arabia, was the site of a lucrative pilgrimage each year. Monotheism would have been received as being incredibly bad for the Meccan economy.

Why do Muslims view Christianity as a polytheistic religion?

Muslims believe Jesus was human, not divine. Christians believe Jesus was God Incarnate, the Son of God, and Savior. Islam views the idea of God having an offspring as heresy (ancient Arabian pagans believed Allah had three daughters). The London School of Theology's text on Islam explains the difference in this manner: "To Muhammad the Christian idea of the Trinity meant worship of three gods, and was simply another form of that polytheism against which he had battled in Mecca" (Cotterell, 31). By definition, Islam teaches that the Christian Trinity includes Mary.

How did Islam spread initially?

It is commonly held that Islam spread primarily by the sword over the first hundred years. David Brown, author of *A Guide to Religions*, adds three additional methods used for the early spread of Islam:

> Muslim traders and merchants traveled from Arabia, practicing Islam in each new land. Many new converts came through these travels. In time Muslim teachers and Holy Men would join these caravans to seek converts and to build mosques and schools. Many of the clerics would remain in the new lands in order to instill Islam into every facet of society. For the most part, the spread of Islam

came through conquest. A Muslim leader would take an area for Islam and *Shari'a* would be implemented. (201–202)

Is the Qur'an the Muslim Bible?

The Arabic word Qur'an means "recitation." The Qur'an is Islam's holy text in that it is Allah's revelation to humankind. The Qur'an, therefore, contains not the words of Muhammad, but the words of Allah. Muhammad received Allah's revelations over twenty-three years, and they were later compiled into the text of the Qur'an. The Qur'an is different from the Hebrew and Christian scriptures in many ways. One in particular is that the Qur'an is first and foremost a text to be memorized and recited, primarily in the original Arabic.

What is abrogation?

Abrogation is unique to the Qur'an among holy texts. Simply put, if a later revelation from Allah contradicted an earlier one, the earlier verse was cancelled or abrogated. The Qur'an is also uniquely formatted, as the longer suras (chapters) are placed first and the shortest last. This lack of any logical or chronological order, combined with abrogation, makes an accurate or precise reading of the Qur'an difficult.

How does a person become a Muslim?

Islam has a profession of faith called the *Shahadah*. A potential convert is required to repeat these words in front of Muslim witnesses: "There is no god but God, and Muhammad is the messenger of God." The first portion makes one a muslim, "a submitter to God. When the second portion is recited one becomes a Muslim, an adherent of the religion of Islam" (Farah, 104).

What is the Islamic concept of sin?

Sin in Islam is intrinsically tied to behavior and actions. Fazlur Rahman states, "The aim of the Qur'an is man and his behavior, not God" (3). Ishak Ghatas expands this point in his academic paper, "Sin and Its Solution to Islam": "In other words the aim of the Qur'an is not to reveal God Himself as much as His laws as man might submit to them in order to live in harmony with Allah and with the cosmic order. Any breaking of Allah's revealed laws is a sin" (3).

Is it true that Muslims earn their salvation?

Yes. Islam is inherently a religion of positive actions that lead to salvation. Judaism and Islam are quite similar in requiring a combination of orthodoxy (right belief) and orthopraxy (right practice). The majority Christian stance requires only right belief for salvation. Muslims are required to adhere to the five pillars and live in submission to Allah. At death Muslims will have their good deeds balanced against their bad deeds, with the final tally determining the eternal destination of either Paradise or Hell.

Do Muslims believe that Paradise and Heaven are the same place?

Islam uses only Paradise to describe the final destination for righteous Muslims, while the Christian New Testament uses both Heaven and Paradise interchangeably. The descriptions of Paradise also differ greatly between Islam and Christianity. Islam teaches a sensual Paradise "of earthly joys where milk and honey, water and wine flow, and the beautiful women of Paradise (*houris*) sweeten eternal life for men" (Machatschke, 13). Christianity teaches a fully spiritual dimension that contains none of the earthly, human commodities. Islam teaches that avoiding the human element, sensuality, and alcohol in this life will lead to an eternity filled with such delights. Traditional Christianity teaches the exact opposite; that overcoming sensuality and carnal desires will lead to an existence devoid of such options.

Why are Muslims required to pray five times per day?

Prayer (*salat*) is one of the five pillars of Islam. Prayer comes after the profession of faith (*shahadah*) in the list, making it the most important act for the Muslim. Frog and Amy Orr-Ewing write, "The general tone of the Qur'an is meditative and somber, because its purpose is to be a dialogue between Allah and humanity. The Five Pillars are an earnest response to Allah. *Salat,* or the daily prayers, serves as a constant reminder of the transitory nature of life" (6). Daily prayers are prescribed for dawn, midday, afternoon, sunset, and before retiring for the night. The praying Muslim is to face in the direction of Mecca. Scheduling prayer times over the course of the day allows for regular submission to Allah.

Why are there two types of Muslims in the world?

There are actually many variations of Muslims today, but the two main types are Sunni and Shi'a. Great cohesion in Islam was a hallmark of Muhammad's time, but schisms began to occur soon after his unexpected death. Muhammad died with no plans for succession in place. Disagreements ensued over who would make the best and most qualified successor. One group favored the long-held Arabic practice of naming a blood relative to succeed Muhammad. This faction nominated Ali, cousin and son-in-law of Muhammad, as first successor. Another group endorsed one of the older, more experienced companions of Muhammad to assume leadership. This group won the vote, and Abu Bakr was selected to succeed Muhammad. Those who favored the family line of succession began to break away from the majority, eventually becoming known as the Party of Ali, or Shi'a in the abbreviated form. Sunni Islam, or Followers of the Path (*Sunnah*), major on the example set by the Prophet and see the next leader as one who best exemplifies Islam, family line notwithstanding. Ali was selected as the Fourth Rightly Guided Caliph, but by that time the schism was undeniable. Shi'a Islam is the minority expression, making up 10 to 15 percent of Muslims.

What is a Sufi Muslim?

Sufism is a mystical, experiential expression of Islam. Eighth-century Sufi mystics reacted against the perceived worldliness of Islam by wearing rough woolen garments. The greatly expanded versions of Islam favored clothes of fine silk and satin (*sufi* is Arabic for "wool"). Maqsood lists the foundational goals of Sufism: "To abandon the desire for worldly wealth and luxury; to search for the inner spiritual life; to achieve union with Allah through direct emotional experience; to move so close to Allah that human consciousness gives way to consciousness of God; to overcome human appetites and desires and the focus on self (131–32). Sufism honors the words of Ali: 'Ascetism is not that you should not own anything, but that nothing should own you.'"

Is Islam really a religion of peace?

Since September 11, 2001, this question has been greatly debated. The president of the United States and the prime minister of Great Britain each stated that Islam is a religion of peace. This came after the hijacking of the planes and the attacks on New York and Washington, DC. If Muslims masterminded the attacks in the US and have been doing much the same in the UK for years, could Islam really be a peaceful religion? The answer is both yes and no. The unique construction of the Qur'an and the gradual evolution of Islam toward a militaristic faith allows for both contrasting extremes in the same religion. Peter Riddell writes, "the answer lies not in an 'either . . . or' response, but rather in a 'both . . . and' one. The Islamic sacred texts offer the potential to be interpreted in both a peaceful and a militaristic way. It depends on how individual Muslims wish to read them" (199). If a Muslim is inclined to cite a command for jihad through war, they can accurately cite the holy books. On the other hand, if a peaceful, more moderate Muslim seeks peace and equality, they too can claim Qur'anic authority.

What do Muslims believe about marriage and divorce?

Marriage is an important element of faith practice for Muslims. In modern Islam, monogamy is the recommended norm, but in the early era multiple wives were common. The Qur'an actually teaches polygyny, marriage to multiple women, rather than polygamy, marriage to multiple spouses. Muslim men are allowed to marry up to four women; Muslim women are not allowed to have more than one spouse simultaneously. Polygyny continues to be practiced in the most conservative Islamic societies, but as a rule the Western approach to marriage is in place for the majority of today's Muslims. Either the husband or the wife may initiate divorce, although it is commonly easier for the man to divorce the wife than the reverse. This, too, has changed in modern societies where *Shari'a* and tradition have given way to secular legal systems. Islam also is unbalanced in regards to mixed marriage; Muslim men may marry non-Muslims, but Muslim women are not allowed the same privilege.

Why are Muslim women required to wear the veil?

Contrary to common belief, Muhammad only required the *hijab* for his family. He conducted business from the family home, and thus many men would be in the company of his wives and children. He instituted a veil, or curtain, to be erected in his home to shield his female family members from the visiting men. He also required the head covering to be worn by his female family when in public. Later jurists and other religious leaders expanded this to apply to all Muslim women when in public. Muslims teach that veiling women is an exercise in modesty and a way for women to promote spirituality over physical attributes. Over time the practice expanded to women covering virtually the entire body in a loose manner in order to fully conceal their natural form. This pursuit of modesty was also put into practice to keep men from committing the sexual sin of lust.

Does Islam permit suicide bombers?

The Qur'an does not directly deal with this topic. In fact, the emergence of this heinous act in the name of religion is relatively new on the world stage. The Qur'an lists only one verse that relates to the taking of one's own life (4:29); however, the Hadith clearly dictates that suicide is forbidden. Esposito reports that both Sunni and Shiite Muslims forbid "sacrificial religious suicide" (125). So why are there weekly attacks by suicide bombers across the Muslim landscape? Modern Muslim extremists have intertwined the notion of martyrdom and the killing of infidels with Allah's ultimate will for Islam. The "House of War" is defined as the portions of the world that have not yet been placed under Islamic control and influence. Extremists see the mass killing of infidels and/or aggressors as a move in the right direction of Islam overall. Add the idea that a suicide bomber is a martyr, and as such will be guaranteed a place in Paradise, and it is easier to fathom why so many Muslims are willing to die for the cause. Braswell highlights the additional factor of family honor tied to *Shahid*: "The Qur'an does provide different rewards for the practice of jihad. They include rewards for punishing non-Muslims and for being a martyr. Martyrdom guarantees a place in paradise and an honorable name bestowed upon one's family (Qur'an 47:4-5)" (38).

Why do some Muslims seem to hate the United States and the West?

This question actually has many answers but can be adequately addressed with two: Israel and the perceived aggression of the United States.

Islam and Judaism share a mutual hatred that goes back to the later time of Muhammad. In reality, the conflict has historical roots in Israel gaining the Promised Land centuries before Muhammad. To this day there are issues over who authentically owns the land shared by Israel and Palestine. Add the United States's seemingly unyielding support of Israel, and it is clear that Islam sees two identifiable enemies (the U.S. *and* Israel). All of this was complicated to a higher degree by the Kuwait war and the Iraq invasion. Muslim theology views the invasion of a Muslim country as act of war against all Islam (*umma*). At this point, Islam feels that America is a double enemy.

Additionally, it is common to hear that Islam sees the West as the "Great Satan" (*Khomeini*) due to both democracy and inherent carnality of our culture. Islam may see us as the "Great Satan," but neither democracy nor carnality is an overriding reason for the obvious divide that exists.

Do Muslims in America have similar attitudes and characteristics to those in predominantly Muslim countries?

According to the epic Pew Research Center study of Muslim Americans, there are approximately 2.35 million Muslims living in America ("Muslim Americans: Middle Class and Mostly Mainstream," 9). These Muslim Americans are largely assimilated into the country and hold similar views on many issues, as do other Americans. Seventy-eight percent say suicide bombings of civilians are never justified to defend Islam. Sixty-five percent of Muslim Americans are foreign born. They believe that Muslims coming to the United States should adopt American customs, rather than trying to remain distinct. Socioeconomically, they are on par with average Americans. Muslims in America oppose the wars in Iraq and Afghanistan. Muslims in America are diverse in the expression of Islam they follow. Fifty percent identify themselves as Sunni; 16 percent identify with the Shi'a sect; and 22 percent describe themselves as simply Muslim with no distinct affiliation. Many Muslim Americans are native-born converts, the majority from Christianity, and the majority of those being African Americans. The entire study is voluminous and exhaustive, and demonstrates that Muslims share many attitudes regardless of location, but that Muslims in America seem to be more assimilated than those in other countries.

What is a Wahhabi Muslim?

Ibn Abd ul-Wahhab lived in the 1700s in Saudi Arabia as an ultra-conservative scholar of Islamic law and theology. Wahhab reacted against the perceived decline in morals and conduct in the societies of Mecca and Medina by calling for a fresh interpretation of Islam and a return to the fundamental era of Muhammad. Wahhab joined with Ibn Saud to unite the Arabian tribes into a puritanical version of Islam, purely black and white, Muslim versus non-Muslim in nature. All nonaligned Muslims who resisted were deemed infidels and were fought against, with most being killed. In a move reminiscent of Muhammad's destruction of the pagan gods of ancient Arabia, Wahhabi forces destroyed the tombs of Muhammad and his companions in Mecca and Medina, plus the shrine to Hussein in Iraq. This incensed the Shi'a population and led to the discord with Wahhabi Sunni Islam that continues to exist. The Wahhabi movement was later defeated, but came back into power in the twentieth century as Saudi Arabia consolidated all of Arabia into a Wahhabi nation. Osama bin Laden is a disciple of Wahhab and used his inspiration in the formation of al-Qaeda.

Who are the Taliban?

The Taliban (from *talib*, meaning "students of religion") formed in the 1960s in Afghanistan from students who sought a modernist Islamic thrust. Early on, the Muslim Youth Movement rallied against Zionism, American politics, and class differences. Over time they became increasingly militant and later were linked with bin Laden's al-Qaeda and attacks on the *USS Cole*, the World Trade Center, U.S. embassies, and the Twin Towers/Pentagon. They also drove the Soviet Union from Afghanistan in what amounted to a bloody and costly defeat for the Soviets. Domestically, this group sought to reestablish a literal Islam based on the Qur'an and to place the entire country under Shari'a. The Taliban has also worked to rid the country of all Shiite Muslims as they are not believed to be following a genuine Islam. To be truthful, Taliban forces have virtually destroyed the country of Afghanistan and rendered life there to the primitive level. They have also regressed in the treatment of women. Outside the Sudan region, Afghanistan is the most regressive and dangerous Islamic land on the planet.

Why should I take the time to understand Islam better?

There has never been a point in the history of religion that is as tenuous as today's. While this can, and likely will, be argued, there is no denying the deadly fragmentation in place between the three main religions of the world. Islam and Judaism are in the process of destroying Palestine solely in order to claim its soil by heavenly mandate. Christianity has a foundation of equality and loving expression, although neither seems to surface when confronting Islam. Militant Islam is exclusivist, even within Islam, and is intent on the removal of Israel from both the Holy Land and the planet—all in the name of God.

Islam is the second fastest-growing religion in the world with 1.2 billion adherents in sixty countries. Christianity is still the largest and fastest-growing religion in a world increasingly shared with Muslims and Jews. If one assumes that Islam and Judaism will continue to be mortal enemies, and that Christianity will continue to coexist peacefully with Israel, the only viable answer lies in a dialogue between Islam and Christianity. It would seem to be wholly unreligious for one faith group to bomb their perceived enemies into oblivion without, at the minimum, giving dialogue a try. Of course, Islam is greatly fragmented and is inherently an ideology of both mosque and state, where Christianity is entirely a religious entity. Islam can be both the church and state simultaneously. This suggests that the best hope for religious dialogue lies with Christianity.

If it is accurate that the average Christian suffers from a functional ignorance of Islam and an aggravated fear of Muslims, the likelihood of dialogue is nil. If the same Christian undertakes a process of understanding Islam that leads to dialogue, the possibility of positive relationships exponentially increases. Genuine understanding can greatly moderate fear and is the only true marker for building relationships. As Van Gorder writes,

> Many Christians have tried to communicate the Gospel without first understanding the Muslim concept of God and perception of Jesus, and this has led to confusion and frustration for both parties. The central theological message for Christians interacting with Muslims is not that "our God" is true and "your God" is not, but the biblical revelation that "God is love" and is actively seeking humanity to participate in a new covenant with God. The revelation that "God is love" cannot be proven, but it can be easily discredited by strident advocacy. (12, 16)

GLOSSARY

Abbasids—The second major dynasty of the Islamic empire that ruled from 750 to the Mongol conquest of Baghdad in 1258.

Ablution—A ritual washing to achieve purity in preparation for various significant events.

Abrogation—The cancellation of a revealed teaching by a later revelation.

Abu Bakr—Early companion of Muhammad and First Rightly Guided Caliph who succeeded the Prophet as leader of Islam.

Aisha—Daughter of Abu Bakr and wife of Muhammad.

Ali—Son-in-law and cousin of Muhammad and Fourth Rightly Guided Caliph; first to be recognized by Shiites.

Allah—Arabic word for God; literally "the god."

Allahu Akbar—"God is great."

Asr—The third daily prayer; afternoon prayer.

Ayat—A verse in the Qur'an.

Ayatollah—Highest level of cleric in Shi'a Islam.

Baraka—Blessing.

Beduoin—Nomadic Arabic tribes.

Bismillah—Arabic for "In the Name of Allah."

Burqa—A garment that covers the female body; veiling.

Caliph—Arabic for "successor," specifically used in Islam for successor of Muhammad.

Chador—Full covering for Iranian female Muslim.

Companions—Early converts who lived in the presence of Muhammad.

Dar al-Harb—Arabic for "House of War."

Dar al-Islam—Arabic for "House of Islam."

Deen—Religious practice, such as fasting, reciting creed, prayer, etc.

Dhimmi—A member of one of the protected religions who lived in a Muslim land as a second-class citizen and paid a tax.

Fajr—The first daily prayer; dawn prayer.

Fatima—Daughter of Muhammad; wife of Ali.

Fatwa—Religious decree.

Faqih—A doctor of the shari'a; canon lawyer.

Fiqh—Jurisprudence; understanding of the law.

Gabriel—The angel through which Allah communicated to Muhammad.

Ghusl—Ritual bathing before prayer.

Hadith—Story of Muhammad; written collection of sayings and examples.

Hafiz—A person who memorizes the Qur'an.

Hajj—Pilgrimage to Mecca; one of the Five Pillars of Islam.

Hajji—One who has made the pilgrimage to Mecca.

Halal—That which is permitted in Islam.

Hanafi—One of four main schools of law in Sunni Islam.

Hanbali—One of the four main schools of law in Sunni Islam.

Hanif—Arabic for a true monotheist.

Haram—That which is forbidden in Islam.

Harim—Household portion for females to which non-related males are not permitted.

Hasan—First son of Ali; grandson of Muhammad; second Shi'a imam.

Hijab—A female's head scarf or head covering.

Hijra—Migration of Muhammad and Muslims from Mecca to Medina in 622 CE.

Hira—Mountain where Muhammad received his first revelation.

Husain—Second son of Muhammad; grandson of Muhammad; third Shi'a imam; killed at Karbala leading to the official split of Islam into Sunni and Shi'a.

Iblis—Arabic and Islamic word for "devil."

Ibn—Arabic for "son of." Also "bin," and abbreviated "b."

Id—Arabic for "feast" or "holiday."

Iftar—Evening meal during Ramadan.

Ijma—Islamic for "consensus."

Imam—Prayer leader for Sunni Islam; legitimate leader of Shi'a Islam.

Insha'Allah—Arabic for "God willing."

Irhab—Terrorism.

Isa—Jesus.

Islam—Surrender or submission to God; an adherent to Muslim religion.

Jahannam—Arabic name for "hell."

Jihad—Struggle to live one's life according to Divine will; "lesser jihad" is to wage holy war against the opponents of Islam.

Jinn—Spirit being that can be either good or bad.

Jizya—Tax to be paid by dhimmis.

Juma—Friday congregational prayer in mosque.

Kaa'bah—Cube-like structure in Mecca; site of pilgrimage.

Kafir—Arabic for "unbeliever." Common to describe non-Muslims.

Kalam—Theology.

Khadijah—Muhammad's first wife; first convert to Islam.

Kharijites—First sectarian group in Islam; fell out with Ali after he accepted arbitration rather than military victory; later one member assassinated Ali.

Madrasa—Islamic religious school.

Maghrib—Fourth prayer of the day; sunset prayer.

Mahdi—Hidden imam who will return near the end of time.

Malak—Angel.

Matn—Text of the Hadith.

Mawali—Non-Arab Muslim.

Mecca—Birthplace of Muhammad and center of polytheistic worship in Arabia.

Medina—Place to which Muhammad and Muslims migrated after leaving Mecca.

Minaret—Mosque prayer tower from which the faithful are called to pray.

Monotheism—Worship of a single god.

Mosque—Place for communal activities; place of prayer and learning.

Mujahidin—A person who fights in a holy war.

Muslim—Adherent of Islam.

Muta—Temporary marriage.

Naskh—Arabic for "abrogation."

Paradise—Place for eternal rewards for Muslims.

PBUH—Acronym for "Peace Be Upon Him," used when referencing a prophet.

People of the Book—Qur'anic term for Jews and Christians.

Qadar—Destiny; the Divine Decree of Allah.

Qibla—The direction of prayer toward Mecca.

Qital—Fighting; allowed in Islam only in self-defense with specific rules.

Qur'an—Revealed text in Islam; literally means "recitation."

Quraysh—Ancestral tribe of Muhammad.

Ramadan—Ninth month of the Muslim calendar; the month of fasting.

Rajm—Capital punishment by stoning.

Salat—Prescribed daily prayers for Muslims.

Sawm—Fasting; one of Five Pillars of Islam.

Shafii—One of four main schools of law in Sunni Islam.

Shahada—Muslim profession of faith; one of Five Pillars of Islam.

Shahid—A martyr for the cause of Allah or Islam.

Shari'a—Islamic law.

Shi'a—"Party of Ali."

Shiite—Adherent of the Shi'a sect of Islam; follower of Party of Ali.

Shirk—Polytheism; associating something with Allah that impugns the Absoluteness of Allah.

Sunnah—Written traditions about Muhammad's example.

Sunni—The majority party of Islam who see the true line of succession from Muhammad to be found in first four caliphs.

Sura—A chapter in the Qur'an; 114 found in Qur'an.

Tahajud—Evening prayers.

Tahrif—Islamic belief that the original text of Bible has been corrupted.

Tawhid—Unity of Allah; denial of the Christian Trinity.

Tawrat—Law of Moses; Torah.

Ulama—Plural of Imam; religious leaders.

Umar—Companion of Muhammad; second successor of the Prophet.

Umma—Worldwide community of Muslims.

Uthman—Companion of Muhammad; third successor of the prophet.

Wahhabi—Ultra-conservative movement centered in Saudi Arabia.

Wudu—Ablution before prayer.

Zabur—Original Psalms of David in corrupted form in the Old Testament.

Zakat—Annual tax on Muslims; typically 2.5 percent; one of the five pillars of Islam.

Zuhr—Second daily prayer; noon prayer.

WORKS CITED

Ajiola, Alhaj. *The Essence of Faith in Islam.* Pakistan: Islamic Publications, 1978.

Ali, Maulana Muhammad. *The Religion of Islam* (revised edition). Dublin OH: Lahore, 2005.

———. *Muhammad the Prophet.* Dublin OH: Lahore 1993.

Andre, Tor. *Mohammad, the Man and his Faith.* Translated by Theophil Menzel. New York: Harper & Row, 1955.

Aslan, Reza. *No god but God.* New York: Harper & Row, 2005.

Armour, Rollin, Sr. *Islam, Christianity and the West: A Troubled History.* New York: Orbis Books, 2002.

Armstrong, Karen. *Islam: A Short History.* New York: Modern Library, 2002.

Barazangi, Nimat Hafez. *Women's Identity and the Qur'an.* Gainesville: University of Florida Press, 2004.

Bowker, John. *What Muslims Believe.* Oxford UK: Oneworld Publications, 1998.

Braswell, George W. *What You Need to Know about Islam & Muslims.* Nashville: Broadman Press, 2000.

Brown, David. *A Guide to Religions.* London: SPCK, 1975.

Bunting, Madeline. "Can Islam Liberate Women?" *London Guardian,* 8 December 2001.

Bushnell, Andrew. "Child Marriage in Afghanistan and Pakistan," *America* 186/8 (11 March 2002) 12–15.

Caner, Emir F., and Ergun M. Caner. *More than a Prophet.* Grand Rapids MI: Kregel, 2003.

———. *Unveiling Islam.* Grand Rapids MI: Kregel, 2002.

Catherwood, Christopher. *Christians, Muslims, and Islamic Rage.* Grand Rapids MI: Zondervan, 2003.

Chapman, Craig. *Cross and Crescent.* Wheaton IL: Tyndale Press, 1989.

Concise Encyclopedia of Islam. San Francisco: HarperCollins, 1991.

Cotterell, Peter. London School of Theology Islam course textbook. London School of Theology, 2002.

Cox, Caroline and John Marks. *The 'West', Islam and Islamism.* London: Civitas, 2003.

Cragg, Kenneth. *The Event of the Qur'an.* London: Allen and Unwin, 1971.

Craig, Kenneth. *Islam and the Muslim.* London: Open University Press, 1978.

Demy, Timothy, and Gary P. Stewart. *In the Name of God: Understanding the Mindset of Terrorism.* Eugene OR: Harvest House, 2002.

Dodge, Christine Huda. *The Everything Understanding Islam Book.* Avon MA: Adams Media, 2003.

Drummond, Richard Henry. *Islam for the Western Mind.* Charlottesville VA: Hampton Roads Publishing, 2005.

Ehlke, Roland C. *Speaking the Truth in Love to Muslims.* Milwaukee: Northwestern Publishing, 2004.

Esposito, John. *What Everyone Needs to Know about Islam.* Oxford: Oxford University Press, 2002.

Farah, Caesar. *Islam, Beliefs and Observances.* Woodbury NY: Barrons Educational Series, 1968.

Galwash, A. A. *The Religion of Islam.* Cairo, Egypt: I'timad Press, 1945.

Geisler, Norman, and Abdul Saleeb. *Answering Islam.* Grand Rapids MI: Baker Books, 1993.

Ghatas, Ishak. "Sin and Its Solution in Islam." Unpublished academic paper. Evangelical Theological Faculty. Leuven, Belgium, 2006.

Haneef, Suzanne. *What Everyone Should Know about Islam and Muslims.* Chicago: Kazi Publishing, 1979.

Hassaballa, Hesham A., and Kabir Helminski. *Beliefnet Guide to Islam.* New York: Three Leaves Press, 2006.

Hewer, C. T. R. *Understanding Islam.* Minneapolis: First Fortress Press, 2006.

Hoffman, Brad. *Inside Terrorism.* New York: Columbia Press, 1998.

Horrie, Chris, and Peter Chippendale. *What Is Islam.* London: Virgin Books, 1991.

Hussain, Amir. *Oil and Water: Two Faiths: One God.* Kelowna, BC Canada: Cooperhouse Publishing, 2006.

Ibrahim, Raymond, ed. and trans. *The Al Qaeda Reader.* New York: Broadway Books, 2007.

Jeurgensmeyer, Mark. *Terror in the Mind of God: The Global Rise of Religious Violence.* Berkeley: University of California Press, 2000.

Khan, Muhammad Z. *Deliverance from the Cross.* London: Southfields, 1978.

Khomeini. *Sayings of the Ayatollah Khomeini.* New York: Bantam, 1980.

Kimball, Charles. *When Religion Becomes Evil.* San Francisco: Harper, 2002.

Lawrence, Bruce. *The Qur'an.* New York: Atlantic Monthly Press, 2006.

Legrain, J. F. 2003 Congressional Testimony. Library of Congress Archives.

———. "Hamas: Legitimate Heir to Palestinian Nationalism?" in John Esposito, editor. *Political Islam.* Boulder: Lynne Rienner Publishing, 1997.

Lewis, Bernard. *The Crisis of Islam.* New York: Random House, 2004.

Lippman, Thomas. *Understanding Islam.* New York: Meridian, 1995.

Lunde, Paul. *Islam.* New York: DK Publishing, 2002.

Machatschke, Roland. *Islam: The Basics.* Canterbury UK: SCM Press, 1995.

Maqsood, Ruqaiyyah W. *Teach Yourself Islam.* London: Contemporary Books, 1994.

"Muslim Americans: Middle Class and Mostly Mainstream." Pew Research Center. 22 May 2007. Available online: http://pewresearch.org/assets/pdf/muslim-americans.pdf (accessed 21 January 2008).

Nasr, Seyyed H. *Islam: Religion, History and Civilization.* San Francisco: Harper, 2003.

Orr-Ewing, Frog, and Amy Orr-Ewing. *Holy Warriors.* London: Authentic Lifestyle Books, 2002.

Parshall, Phil. *Understanding Muslim Teachings and Traditions.* Grand Rapids MI: Baker Books, 1994.

Peters, Rudolph. *Jihad in Classical and Modern Islam.* Princeton: M. Weimer Publishing, 1966.

Pipes, Daniel. *In the Path of God: Islam and Political Power.* New York: Basic Books, 1983.

Powell, Bill. "Struggle for the Soul of Islam." *Time* 164/11 (14 September 2004). Available online: http://www.time.com/time/magazine/article/0,9171,1101040913-692840,00.html (accessed 21 January 2008).

Rahman, Fazlur. *Major Themes of the Qur'an.* Minneapolis: Chicago Press, 1983.

Reisacher, Evelyne A. "Beyond the Veil." *Christian Reflection: A Series in Faith in Ethics.* Ed. The Center for Christian Ethics, Baylor University. Volume 15 (April 2005): 76–83.

Renard, John. *Responses to 101 Questions on Islam.* New York: Paulist Press, 1998.

Riddell, Peter G., and Peter Cotterell. *Islam in Conflict: Past, Present and Future.* Leicester UK: IVP, 2003.

Riddell, Peter. *Christians and Muslims.* Leicester UK: IVP, 2004.

Roraback, Amanda. *Islam in a Nutshell.* Santa Monica CA: Enisen Publishing, 2002.

Sarder, Ziauddin, and Zafir Malik. *Introducing Islam.* Roystan UK: Tutenbooks, 2004.

Spencer, Robert. *Islam Unveiled.* San Francisco: Encounter Books, 2002.

———. *The Truth about Mohammed.* Washington DC: Regnery Publishing, 2006.

Waddy, Charis. *The Muslim Mind.* London & New York: Longman Press, 1976.

Watt, Montgomery. *Muhammad at Medina.* Oxford UK: Clarendon Press, 1956.

———, ed. *Bell's Introduction to the Qur'an.* Edinburgh: University of Edinburgh Press, 1970.

———. *Early Islam.* Edinburgh: University of Edinburgh Press, 1990.

Wensinck, A. J. *A Handbook of Early Muhammadan Tradition.* Leiden UK: Brill, 1960.

———. *The Muslim Creed.* Cambridge: University Press, 1965.

Van Gorder, A. Christian. "No God But God: Theological Currents in Contemporary Muslim-Christian Relations." *Christian Reflection: A Series in Faith in Ethics.* Ed. The Center for Christian Ethics, Baylor University. Volume 15 (April 2005): 11–17.